The Ebony Success Library

The Ebony Success Library

Volume III
Career Guide

Opportunities and Resources for You

By the Editors of Ebony

The Southwestern Company,
Nashville, Tenn.
By arrangement with
Johnson Publishing Company Inc., 1973

Copyright © 1973 by Johnson Publishing Company, Inc.
Chicago, Illinois

All rights reserved, including the right to reproduce
this book or portion thereof in any form.

Printed in the United States of America

Library of Congress Cataloguing in Publication Data

Main entry under title:
Career guide: opportunities and resources for you.

(The Ebony success library, v. 3)
1. Negroes—Employment.   I. Ebony.   II. Series.
E185.8.C36   1973   331.7'02   73-5723
ISBN 0-87485-062-2

R.R.D. 1-73

Publisher
John H. Johnson

Editor
Charles L. Sanders

Designer
Cecil L. Ferguson

Production Coordinator
Brenda M. Biram

Production Assistants
Editorial: Brenda J. Butler
Photographs: Basil O. Phillips

Introduction

Finishing high school is a milestone for many young black people, but once the celebration is over, those who have not made further plans are confronted with the question, "What will I do now?" *Career Guide: Opportunities and Resources for You* is designed to help answer that question. It is also planned as a reference for students who may want to plan their high school studies (and advanced education) with a particular field in mind.

A significant part of successful career planning is to have the skills that are in demand when one's training is completed. Thus we have highlighted many careers whose growth will demand many new employees over the next several years. Some of the fields that are very popular today—radio and television, newspapers and magazine journalism, advertising and photography—seem very glamorous, but the demand for employees in such fields is not expected to increase during the 1970s. Furthermore, competition for the few available opportunities is intense. Possibly one will find an allied field among those we list with good future possibilities. A starting position in a related career may facilitate transfer, after some experience has been gained, into a field with fewer opportunities at entry level.

We suggest that the reader carefully study the table of contents before turning to any particular career. Perhaps it will be useful to consider several careers before settling on one.

Some students for whom college is not a possibility should refer to *Careers Without College*, where we list about thirty occupations, some requiring training that is available in high schools or vocational schools. There is an extensive section on *Medical and Health-Related Careers* covering areas that need trained personnel to meet growing health-care demands. We stress here and throughout the book that readers should write to the addresses listed or take all questions not answered here to a guidance counselor, teacher or principal. They are there to help you get all the facts.

Since money is part of the total picture, we have also included a section on *Scholarships and Financial Aid*. There, it is almost guaranteed, scholarships and/or loans will be found that suit your career plans.

In compiling this volume, we have been given the aid and advice of numerous individuals, organizations and business firms. We gratefully acknowledge the assistance of the United States Department of Labor for providing information in its *Occupational Outlook Handbook*. And special thanks go to Ed Wieland of the American Legion for permitting us to use as a resource the Legion's excellent student handbook *Need A Lift?* A very valuable contribution was made by Dr. Andrew L. Thomas, director of the National Medical Association's

"Project 75," whose staff assisted in the compilation of the section on *Medical and Health-Related Careers*. Miss Deborah Lee gave us many hours of invaluable service as special editorial assistant. And certainly we are grateful to all of the persons who permitted us to spotlight the success they have achieved in their many and varied careers. We hope that, for the thousands of young people who will use this volume as a reference, we have made less difficult the task of choosing a career.

The Editors of Ebony

Contents

Careers and People

Wesley C. Agnew
Product Engineering Draftsman

Wesley C. Agnew is a product engineering draftsman with American Motors Corporation, Detroit, Michigan. He prepares drawings of newly designed or revised parts for use by tool and die shops and production plants. The drawings can vary in size from 8 by 10-inch sheets to 10 by 15-foot paper rolls.

Mr. Agnew took detailing courses at the H.L. Bosca School of Automotive Design. He also studied geometry at the Applied Management and Technology Center of Wayne State University. Starting as a clerk at American, he has been promoted three times on the way to his present position.

Speaking on opportunities for blacks in the field, he says: "There is still room for more blacks to be hired as draftsmen. There are only two blacks in my department, but I think opportunities for blacks in the body engineering field are expanding as the doors open and the barriers fall, and as we educate ourselves for the various jobs."

An activist in his community, Mr. Agnew works with Junior Achievement and a career guidance panel with American Motors. Very much interested in guidance, he says he is against the theory of teaching kids on the assumption that they will attend college. "I think this is wrong because most children don't go to college but think that to get a good job you need a college education. This isn't always true. We should see that young people have an opportunity to attend trade and technical schools, because there are many good positions which do not require a college education."

Mr. Agnew is married and has two children. He enjoys fishing, sports and cars in his spare time.

Career Information

Training

Young persons interested in becoming draftsmen can acquire the necessary training from a number of sources, including technical institutes, junior and community colleges, extension divisions of universities, vocational and technical high schools and correspondence schools. Others may qualify for draftsmen jobs through on-the-job training programs combined with part time schooling or three- or four-year apprenticeship programs. The study of shop practices and the learning of some shop skills are also helpful, since many higher level drafting jobs require knowledge of manufacturing or construction methods.

Outlook

Employment opportunities for draftsmen are expected to be favorable. Prospects will be the best for those having post-high school drafting training. Well-qualified high school graduates who have had only high school drafting will also be in demand for some types of jobs.

Additional Source Material

American Institute for Design and Drafting
P. O. Box 2955
Tulsa, OH 74101

American Federation of Technical Engineers
1126 16th Street, N. W.
Washington, DC 20036

Carlos B. Alexander

Cost Accountant

Carlos B. Alexander is a cost accountant at R. J. Reynolds Industries, Inc. in Winston-Salem, North Carolina. He reviews raw material purchases, keeps cost information concerning plants and analyzes problem areas concerning material usage.

A graduate of the University of Dayton, Ohio, with a B.A. degree and Washington University with an M.B.A. degree, Mr. Alexander says that blacks in accounting, especially internal accounting, are rare and that the opportunities will increase. "The area demands people with empathy; people capable of clear, concise thought coupled with technical skills, and I believe many blacks fit that category."

Mr. Alexander, who is married, says that one of his most significant achievements was his election as president of Student Involvement for Tennessee, which supervised voter registration drives and student groups working in that state.

Born July 30, 1947 in Cleveland, Ohio, Mr. Alexander expected "problems" when he moved to the South. "But they did not materialize, and now I'm sure many of the opportunities for skilled blacks will be in the South," he says.

Cycling, Junior Achievement, toastmastering and being
a small business advisor take up his spare time.

Career Information

Training
Cost accounting is a subfield in the broader accounting field.
In spite of the large number of sources for obtaining an accounting
education, a bachelor's degree with a major in accounting or a
closely related field is increasingly an asset. For advancement
to better positions, it may be required. Candidates having a
master's degree in accounting as well as college training in
other business and liberal arts subjects are preferred by many
firms. The cost accountant might conceivably have training in
engineering or a science in cases where he or she is employed
in an industry that offers highly technical goods or services. In
any case, the accountant, no matter what the specialty, must
be firmly knowledgeable of the company's operating procedures.

Outlook
Accounting employment is expected to expand very rapidly
during the decade because of greater use of accounting information
in business management, complex and changing tax systems, the
growth in size and number of corporations expected to provide
financial reports to stockholders, and the increasing use of
accounting services by small business organizations.

Additional Source Material
National Association of Accountants
505 Park Avenue
New York, NY 10022

National Society of Public Accountants
1717 Pennsylvania Avenue, NW
Washington, DC 20006

Financial Executives Institute
50 W. 44th Street
New York, NY 10036

The Institute of Internal Auditors, Inc.
170 Broadway
New York, NY 10038

John Henry Allen

Group Leader, Development Engineering

John Henry Allen is a group engineer for Lockheed Aircraft Company in Burbank, California. He supervises a team of engineers in development of computer program control test sets that automatically isolate faults in electronic equipment. He was chosen to head the staff of eighteen by a department engineer selected from a pool of senior engineers. He gained experience in the aircraft field by holding positions of senior electronic systems engineer and senior electrical research engineer.

A graduate of Los Angeles State College with a bachelor of science, and of California State College with a master's degree, both in engineering, Mr. Allen feels that there are too few black engineering students. He estimates that only one out of two-hundred blacks hold positions similar to his, and that only one out of fifty engineering students is black.

Mr. Allen is "very optimistic" about future opportunities for blacks in engineering. He says that there are "no limitations in engineering." Although he says the aerospace engineering future is "questionable," the future of computer systems engineering is "unlimited."

Responsible for planning and developing the fabrication and installation of integration test facilities for two separate aircraft models, Mr. Allen says that "once the art of problem solving is discovered one learns that this art has universal application from repairing a sewing machine to troubleshooting an aircraft electronic system."

Born January 16, 1938 in Youngstown, Ohio, Mr. Allen is married and enjoys bicycling and toastmaster projects in his spare time.

Career Information

Training

A bachelor's degree in engineering is the generally accepted educational requirement for entrance into engineering positions. Many large companies have special programs to acquaint new engineers with special industrial practices and to determine the specialty for which they are best suited. All fifty states and the District of Columbia license those engineers whose work may affect life, health or property, or who offer their services to the public. Generally, registration requirements include graduation from an accredited engineering curriculum plus at least four years of experience and the passing of a state examination. Those electrical engineers engaged in research, development and design activities take additional training in their fields of specialization.

Outlook

Opportunities for electrical engineers are expected to increase very rapidly through the seventies. An increased demand for electrical equipment (such as computers and sensing devices to control production processes automatically) is expected to be the major factor contributing to this growth.

Additional Source Material

Institute of Electrical and Electronic Engineers
345 E. 47th Street
New York, NY 10017

Douglass L. Alligood
Corporate Advertising Manager

Douglass L. Alligood is manager of corporate advertising at Radio Corporation of America in New York, New York. He plans, develops and implements RCA's corporate advertising program and supervises activities of J. Walter Thompson Co. and UniWorld Group, Inc. (the two advertising agencies that handle the RCA account) in the preparation of his company's advertising strategies, plans, budgets and copy. Mr. Alligood formerly was an account executive at Batten, Barton, Durstine and Osborn, Inc., a New York advertising agency, where he worked on Dodge, Pepsi-Cola, Auto-Lite and Schaefer Beer accounts. He was born February 15, 1934 in St. Louis, Missouri. He has a bachelor of fine arts degree (with a major in commercial art) from Bradley University.

8

Prospects in advertising are good, "providing general advertising agencies continue to open more account management jobs to blacks, and providing that the new black owned and operated agencies continue to grow and prosper," he says.

Mr. Alligood is a Little League baseball coach and a photographer in his spare time. He and his wife, Cynthia, have four children: Donna, Craig, Debra and Douglass Jr.

Career Information

Training
Advertising manager is another in the array of advertising positions that are becoming available to blacks. Despite the fact that there is no typical educational background for success in advertising, most employers prefer college graduates with liberal arts degrees and majors in advertising, marketing, journalism or business administration. Employees having initiative, drive and talent may progress from beginning jobs to creative, research or managerial work. Management positions require experience in all phases of advertising.

Outlook
Employment of advertising workers is expected to increase slowly through the 1970s. Opportunities should be favorable, however, for highly qualified applicants, especially in advertising agencies as more and more advertisers turn their work over to agencies. Most openings—several thousand a year—are a result of normal occupational attrition, and young people seeking entry positions will face stiff competition.

Additional Source Material
American Advertising Federation
1225 Connecticut Avenue, NW
Washington, DC 20036

American Association of Advertising Agencies
200 Park Avenue
New York, NY 10017

Association of Industrial Advertisers
41 E. 42nd Street
New York, NY 10017

Carlton Leon Anderson

College Relations Consultant

Carlton L. Anderson is a college relations consultant at Prudential Insurance Company of America in Newark, New Jersey. He assists the manager of college relations in recruiting, selecting and placing college graduates in Prudential's home office and in its eastern home office.

A former personnel consultant and claims approver at Prudential, Mr. Anderson was recruited for his present job after resigning from military service. After graduating from Virginia State College with a B.S. degree in biology, he served in

the U.S. Army for six years, resigning as a captain. He was born January 12, 1942 in Ashland, Virginia. He is single, lives in East Orange, New Jersey, and enjoys reading, tennis and photography.

Career Information

Training
College relations consulting is a highly specialized function of the personnel department and, as with most professions requiring a high level of specialization, a college degree in personnel management is regarded favorably by potential employers. Jobs requiring counselling sometimes demand a B.S. degree with a major in psychology or other behavioral science. Companies offer orientation programs for greater familiarization with that particular firm's procedures.

Outlook
College graduates who enter personnel work are expected to find many opportunities throughout the 1970s. Although employment prospects probably will be best for college graduates who have specialized training in personnel administration, positions will be available for those with degrees in other fields. Opportunities for young people to advance from production, clerical or sub-professional jobs to personnel positions will be limited.

Additional Source Material
American Society for Personnel Administration
19 Church Street
Berea, OH 44017

Information About Government Careers
Public Personnel Association
1313 E. 60th Street
Chicago, IL 60637

Harry C. Anderson Jr.

Manager, Financial Planning and Control

Harry C. Anderson Jr. is manager of financial planning control at Audio Magnetics Corporation, a subsidiary of Mattel, Inc., in Gardena, California. He is responsible for profit planning and forecasting, capital budgeting and review, cost control and price estimating. He was promoted after two years as a senior financial analyst at Mattel, a leading manufacturer of toys. The Audio Magnetic Corporation subsidiary is the world's largest manufacturer of audio tapes and tape cassettes.

Born July 3, 1941 in Kingston, Jamaica, Mr. Anderson graduated *summa cum laude* from Fordham University with a B.S. degree in economics and philosophy and was an Alpha Kappa Psi Distinguished Scholar. He feels that future opportunities in his field depend on "the firm's attitude, technical competence of the individual and his ability to handle the politics of U.S. business."

Mr. Anderson and his wife, Audrey, have four children: Gregory, Paula, Lisa and Andrea. They live in Carson, California. He plays chess and is interested in jazz and classical music.

Career Information

Training
Financial planning and control is a field within the general category of economics. Economists need a thorough background in economic theory and methods of economic analysis. A bachelor's degree with a major in economics and a minor in mathematics and/or statistics provides an excellent foundation for entry into financial planning. There are few if any entries into this field without college training. Advanced degrees are required for teaching positions and private industry research positions of high responsibility. Most colleges and universities in the United States offer undergraduate and graduate programs in economics.

Outlook
Employment of economists is expected to increase rapidly through the 1970s. Colleges and universities (which require an advanced degree) will need hundreds of new instructors annually to handle an anticipated rapid increase in enrollment. Openings for economists in industry are expected to increase rapidly also as businessmen become more accustomed to relying on scientific methods of analyzing business trends, forecasting sales and planning purchasing and production operations. At the federal, state and local levels, employment is expected to spiral to meet the need for more extensive data collection and analysis and to provide staff for programs aimed at reducing poverty and unemployment.

Additional Source Material
American Economic Association
1313 21st Avenue, South
Nashville, TN 37212

The International Developer (Economist)
Professional Talent Search
Office of Personnel and Manpower
Agency for International Development
Washington, DC 20523

Lee A. Archer Jr.
Equal Opportunities Director

Lee A. Archer Jr. is director of equal opportunity affairs at General Foods Corporation in White Plains, New York, and is president of North Street Capital Corporation, a General Foods subsidiary in Harrison, New York. At General Foods, Mr. Archer is responsible for the company's compliance with all government equal opportunity programs. He monitors and operates various training programs, and advises company officials on policy development and administration of programs affecting minorities and women. He also oversees the company's voluntary training and scholarship programs and maintains relations with civic, social, civil rights and professional minority groups. The presidency of the North Street Capital Corporation requires him to supervise operations for providing venture capital and technical assistance to minority and other small businesses.

Mr. Archer has a B.S. degree in political science from the University of California at Los Angeles and an M.A. degree in international affairs from New York University. He has studied for a Ph.D. degree at NYU.

Mr. Archer believes that opportunities in the fields of equal opportunity management and minority business are excellent, despite fierce competition. He is a member of the Urban League, NAACP and the National Association of College Professors. He and his wife, Ina, have three sons, Lee III, Raymond and Roy, and a daughter, Ina Diane.

Career Information

Training
Management positions in minority affairs and equal employment opportunities often include other corporate responsibilities such as internal training programs, community relations and minority community programs. All these responsibilities require experience, particularly that gained in rising through successive management levels. Entry is determined by the applicant's experience, such as personnel or office management, finance, economics or accounting. College degrees in these fields are good foundation for entry-level jobs. (See *Training* under other management occupations.)

Outlook
Generally speaking, management trainees will find ample employment opportunities, but those with college training are the best candidates Minority affairs responsibilities will continue as long as the government establishes guidelines for which compliance must be monitored. Other functions in this department—community relations and internal education programs—are likely to continue and to expand with the growth of industry.

Additional Source Material
The American Management Association
135 W. 50th Street
New York, NY 10020

Society for Advancement of Management
1412 Broadway
New York, NY 10036

Bennie Ray Austin

Controller

Bennie Ray Austin is controller at the genetics division of the Carnation Company, in Los Angeles, California. He has control of all accounting, budgeting and financial statements, and supervises the handling of miscellaneous checks and the distribution of government bonds. His division conducts research in dairy and beef herd breeding.

Born November 10, 1943 in Douglassville, Texas, Mr. Austin has a B.A. degree in business administration from Prairie View A&M College. He also has completed the Alexander Hamilton Institute correspondence course in business management.

Mr. Austin feels that, while the number of blacks employed by large corporations as accountants and managers has been on the increase in the last few years, few blacks hold responsible, challenging positions. He says, however, that with a degree in business, accounting or a related field, the opportunities for financial rewards and managerial positions are unlimited.

Mr. Austin and his wife, Bobbie, have two children, Ronitta and Anthony. They live in Mission Hills, California.

Career Information

Training

Controllers are among the vast and ever-growing pool of business administration employees. In general, they have far-ranging responsibilities involving corporate finances. The position requires a strong educational background. Training for entry-level positions (accounting) can be obtained in universities, four-year colleges, junior colleges, accounting and private business schools and correspondence schools. Graduates of all such institutions are included in the ranks of successful accountants. However, a bachelor's degree with a major in accounting or a closely related field is an asset. For advancement, and for the better starting positions, it may be required. Beginners in management accounting may start as ledger accountants or junior internal auditors, or as trainees for technical accounting positions. They may rise to chief cost accountant or budget director, or a comparable position. Accountants who want to get to the top of their profession find it necessary to continue their study of accounting and related problems.

Outlook

Accounting employment is expected to expand very rapidly during the 1970s because of such factors as the greater use of accounting information in business management, complex and changing tax systems, the growth in size and number of corporations required to provide financial reports for stockholders, and the increasing use of accounting services by small business operations. Demand for college-trained accountants will be greater than that for persons without an academic background. However, graduates of business and other schools offering thorough training should also have good job futures. In addition, the trend toward specialization is creating excellent opportunities for persons trained in a specific phase of accounting.

Additional Source Material

National Association of Accountants
505 Park Avenue
New York, NY 10022

Financial Executives Institute
50 W. 44th Street
New York, NY 10036

National Society of Public Accountants
2717 Pennsylvania Avenue, NW
Washington, DC 20006

Theodore P. Avery
Electronic Engineer

Theodore P. Avery is a senior electrical engineer at North American Rockwell Corporation of Los Angeles, California, manufacturers of aerospace, automotive, electronic and industrial parts. Among his contributions is the design of a method for automatically correcting computer tapes that control production of tool and die machines. Mr. Avery is also a consultant on facilities for industrial engineering functions (effective uses of manpower, machines and materials) at the Los Angeles aerospace division.

While Mr. Avery earned a bachelor's degree in electrical engineering from the University of California at Los Angeles in 1944, he started at North American Rockwell as a janitor. That he had electronics knowledge came to light when a supervisor witnessed Mr. Avery rescuing an electrician from electrocution. He has moved up through the ranks to his present position as senior electrical engineer.

Mr. Avery estimates that future opportunities in his field are excellent. "Increasingly intense competition for qualified personnel will open doors heretofore closed to minorities—if they are qualified," he said. He added that statistical evidence of racial prejudice has been significantly reduced.

Born in 1913, in Boley, Oklahoma, Mr. Avery is married. He and his wife Mozelle have four children. His chief leisure interest is fishing.

Career Information

Training

In the four-year curriculum, engineers in this field opt for specialization in electronics in the last two years. The basic entry requirement is a bachelor's degree. Engineering graduates usually begin to work as trainees or assistants to experienced workers. Advanced training is now more frequently emphasized for some jobs. Graduate degrees are desirable for beginning teaching and research positions. Furthermore, some specialties, such as nuclear engineering, are available only at the graduate level. A student should investigate college curricula thoroughly before making a selection.

Outlook

Employment opportunities for electrical engineers are expected to increase very rapidly through the '70s. An increased demand for electrical equipment to automate production processes is expected to be among the major factors contributing to this growth. The anticipated spiraling demand for electrical and electronic consumer goods also is expected to create many job openings for electrical engineers.

Additional Source Material

Institute of Electrical and Electronic
Engineers
345 E. 47th Street
New York, NY 10017

Lawrence R. Banks Jr.
Consumer Affairs Manager

Lawrence R. Banks Jr. is manager of consumer affairs at Avon Products Inc. in New York, New York. He is responsible for proposing, developing and implementing programs relating to individual consumers and organized consumer movements, and for proposing steps to build and maintain consumers' positive attitudes toward the company. He also directs a consumer information center and makes personal appearances on behalf of the company, a leading manufacturer and distributor of cosmetics and toiletries. Its 1971 gross was $875 million.

    Mr. Banks gained experience as a research director, administrative assistant, and account executive with a public relations firm. He also attended the Boston University School of Public Relations and Communications, and has participated in seminars in public relations and management sponsored by the Publicity Club of New York, the Public Relations Society of America, the New York University

School of Continuing Education and Extension Services, and the
University of Michigan Graduate School of Business Administration.

He feels that opportunities for blacks in the field of corporate
public relations will increase.

Because he has little formal education (he is a high school
dropout), Mr. Banks is proud of his level of achievement. He wants to
be a "model for youngsters with whom I come in contact."

He was born October 7, 1927 in Washington, D.C. Divorced, he has
a daughter, Licia, and a son, Lawrence.

Career Information

Training
Consumer affairs is a fairly new occupation that has arisen to meet
the demand from the buying public for greater accountability
by manufacturers. Consumer affairs managers combine many features
of the marketing researcher with public relations, so training in both
areas—in some cases through a degree program—is fast becoming a
requirement with prospective employers. A bachelor's degree is the
usual prerequisite to become a market research trainee, and a master's
degree in business administration is becoming increasingly desirable.
Many people qualify for research jobs through previous experience in
related marketing fields. Courses considered valuable are marketing,
statistics, English composition, speech, psychology, sociology and
economics. The public relations aspect requires courses in journalism,
public relations or English. As of 1973, some twenty colleges offered
degree programs in public relations, and eighteen colleges offered
graduate degrees. At least three hundred colleges offer some public
relations courses.

Outlook
Rapid growth is expected through the remainder of the decade. As the
consumer maintains levels of buying awareness, firms are going to be
called upon to offer such a service.

Additional Source Material
The Information Center
Public Relations Society of America, Inc.
845 Third Avenue
New York, NY 10022

Service Department, Public Relations News
127 E. 80th Street
New York, NY 10021

Joyce M. Bembry

Polymer Patents Advisor

Joyce M. Bembry is advisor on polymeric patents at E. I. du Pont de Nemours and Company in Wilmington, Delaware. She advises the company and supervises search set ups for patents using applications of polymer chemistry. The searches involve the patent literature both in a computerized system and in manual systems including those of the U. S. Patent Office. She identifies the important parts of patents so that they can be indexed, prepares abstracts of patents, edits the indexing and abstracting prepared by her six-member staff and supervises and screens computer searches of the indexed material. Recruited from college, she joined du Pont in 1964 as a patent analyst and was promoted to her present position in 1967. As the first black hired in her department, Miss Bembry feels that her professional work paved the way for other black people to join the staff. In her opinion, opportunities in her field are now very good for blacks.

Born September 15, 1944 in Elko, Georgia, Miss Bembry has a degree in chemistry from Hampton Institute. She is a member of the American Chemical Society and the National Hampton Alumni Association. She lives in Newark, Delaware, and enjoys sewing, reading and travel.

Career Information

Training

After obtaining a bachelor's degree in chemistry, it is possible to branch into any of a number of job situations. Some chemists work as marketing experts or sales representatives of chemical companies and other manufacturers where the employee must be familiar with chemistry-related aspects of products. Most chemists having just the bachelor's degree begin their careers in industry or government. In industry, employers often have special training programs for new chemistry graduates. These programs supplement college training with specific industry techniques and help determine the type of work for which the new employee is best suited. In the case of advisory positions on patents, a thorough knowledge of patent law is required along with academic training in the area of specialization.

Outlook

The employment outlook for chemists is expected to be favorable through the 1970s. In addition to new opportunities resulting from rapid growth especially in research and development, thousands of new chemists will be needed each year to replace those lost through occupational turnover.

Additional Source Material

American Chemical Society
1155 16th Street, NW
Washington, DC 20036

Manufacturing Chemists' Association, Inc.
1825 Connecticut Avenue, NW
Washington, DC 20009

Thomas H. Best
Product Development Engineer

Thomas H. Best is a product development engineer at American Motors Corporation in Detroit, Michigan. He is assistant supervisor in the laboratory in which fuels and lubricants are tested and evaluated. He joined the company in 1965 as a chemical analyst and was promoted in 1971.

Mr. Best is a graduate of South Carolina State College (B.S., biology and chemistry, 1950). He says that the future holds great opportunities in his field for blacks "because there surely will be new areas of research for people with a scientific background."

He and his wife, Patricia, have four children. His hobbies include sports, family trips and working with young people. An active participant in company-sponsored Junior Achievement programs and in Boy Scouts of America, his advice is to "prepare yourself while you're young for the work you will do in your mid-life so that when you're old you can live in peace."

Career Information

Training
(See educational requirements listed under *Training* in other engineering careers.)

Outlook
The outlook is for moderate growth of employment in chemical engineering through the 1970s. The major factors underlying this expected growth are expansion of the industry and continued high expenditures in research and development in which a large number of chemical engineers are employed. Chemical engineers will also be needed in many relatively new areas of work such as environmental control and the design and development of nuclear reactors.

Additional Source Material
American Institute of Chemical Engineers
345 E. 47th Street
New York, NY 10017

Wendell Bodden
Cooperative Education Administrator

Wendell N. Bodden is administrator of cooperative education and high school work-study programs for Grumman Aerospace Corporation in Bethpage, New York. The main objective of the program, which serves nearly three hundred people, is to insure that employees are trained to rise to the maximum level possible within their working assignments at Grumman. Mr. Bodden also counsels the students and monitors their educational progress.

A former designer for Grumman, Mr. Bodden attended C. W. Post College, Greenvale, New York, in preparation for his present position. He received his design training at the New York School of Electronics.

Mr. Bodden was born March 3, 1930 in New York City; he and his wife Natalie have three children: Mark, Wendell and Ingrid. Mr. Bodden is active in voter registration and other community action programs.

26

Career Information

Training

Cooperative education programs established by companies serve, first, to aid the employee in increasing his or her education, and, second, to increase the skill pool within the company. The person who administers such a program can rise to his position through the ranks after years of experience and familiarity with the company's procedures. For young persons seeking careers as management level entrants into such a field, a college degree in business administration, personnel management or industrial management is highly desirable.

Outlook

The proliferation of company educational programs should continue through the 1970s. The employment of salaried managers is likely to increase rapidly because large firms tend to depend more on trained management specialists as they further increase in size. Consequently, the outlook is more favorable for the properly trained.

Additional Source Material

The American Management Association
135 W. 50th Street
New York, NY 10020

Society for Advancement of Management
1412 Broadway
New York, NY 10036

Bruce L. Bozeman

Division Counsel

Bruce L. Bozeman, division counsel at the Birds Eye Division of
General Foods Corporation in White Plains, New York, is responsible
for all legal matters—anti-trust and trade regulations, food and drug
acts, contracts, advertising matters, etc.—relating to the Birds Eye
Division and three division subsidiaries. Birds Eye is one of the nation's
largest frozen food manufacturers; its annual sales are $2.4 billion.
Previously, Mr. Bozeman was assistant counsel for the Maxwell House,
Post, Jell-O and Kool-Aid divisions of General Foods. He was born
January 21, 1944 in Philadelphia, Pennsylvania, and has a B.A. degree
from Virginia Union University and a J.D. degree from Howard University
Law School. He is a member of the bars of New York and the District of
Columbia. Mr. Bozeman feels that opportunities for black corporate
lawyers are increasing. He and his wife, Patricia, have two children,
Herman and Leslie.

28

Career Information

Training
Corporate law subdivides into many areas, among them labor law, tax, trade and contract. Corporate lawyers must maintain a special awareness of developments in their areas of specialization in order to serve their companies in the best manner possible. After four years of college and three years at an accredited law school, corporate lawyers attend seminars, conferences and courses to keep up to date.

Outlook
Opportunities are best in large metropolitan areas where the major employers of corporate lawyers—industry and government—are headquartered. Entry level positions are most easily obtained by graduates of highly regarded institutions or those at the head of their classes. Graduates of less prominent schools or those with a lower scholastic ranking may have to gain experience in the much larger number of law-related occupations.

Additional Source Material
Information Service
American Bar Association
1155 E. 60th Street
Chicago, IL 60637

Association of American Law Schools
1 Dupont Circle, NW, Suite 370
Washington, DC 20036

Richard Brent Jr.
Safety Inspector

Richard Brent Jr. is a safety inspector with Atlantic and Gulf Stevedores, Inc., in New Orleans, Louisiana. He oversees compliance with federal health and safety regulations for the company's longshoremen serving the Gulf South Maritime Ports. During peak shipping periods, as many as one thousand longshoremen and their superintendents come under his supervision.

At one time, Mr. Brent was a winch operator with his company. He has attended Delgado Junior College, in New Orleans, for a degree in industrial safety. He was born April 9, 1940 in New Orleans.

Mr. Brent assesses future possibilities in industrial safety as very good for blacks with the appropriate educational background.

He and his wife, Rosa, have three children: Angel, Toni and Richard.

Career Information

Training

In some cases, training for a position as an industrial technician qualifies interested persons for safety inspection. Generally speaking, young men and women who wish to prepare for careers as engineering or science technicians can obtain the necessary training from a great variety of educational institutions or can qualify for their work right on the job. Specialized formal training is offered in post-secondary schools—technical institutes, junior and community colleges, area vocational-technical schools, and extension divisions of four-year colleges. Engineering and science technicians usually begin work as trainees or in routine positions under experienced technicians, scientists or engineers. As they gain experience, they are given more responsibility.

Outlook

Employment opportunities for engineering and science technicians is expected to be very good during the 1970s. The demand will be greatest for graduates of technician training programs. The continuing growth of science research and development will call for more scientists and, likewise, more technicians to assist them.

Additional Source Material
National Council of Technical Schools
1835 K Street, NW
Washington, DC 20006

American Society for Engineering Education
Suite 400
1 Dupont Circle
Washington, DC 20036

Richard M. Brown

Insurance Company Counsel

Richard McGlenard Brown is counsel for Aetna Life and Casualty in Hartford, Connecticut. He is responsible for legal matters involving Aetna Group Insurance operations, pension tax, mutual fund and profit-sharing plans. He is also on a three-man committee that is responsible for administering and interpreting the Aetna Incentive Savings Profit-Sharing Plan for the company's employees. He wrote the plan and was instrumental in obtaining approval from the Internal Revenue Service.

Mr. Brown was promoted after three years as an Aetna attorney. He has a B.S. degree in political science from the University of San Francisco (1962) and a J.D. degree from Harvard Law School (1968). He is an incorporator and active member of Ujima, Inc., a non-profit minority economic development corporation in Hartford. He is also a member of the American Bar Association and the Harvard Law School Association. He is a member of the Commission of Hartford. He and his wife, Irene, have a son, Richard.

Career Information

Training

A law degree requires a minimum of three years law study beyond the bachelor's degree. The student's choice of specialization determines the course of study throughout those years. For pre-law students, English, history, economics and other social sciences, logic and public speaking are important bases. The student who chooses corporate law and secures an entry level position in a corporation may opt for closer specialization by taking additional courses of study in the appropriate area.

Outlook

Law is highly competitive. Courtroom law requires the lawyer to pass the bar examination in the state where he wishes to practice.
The outlook for private practice is best in small and suburban communities. Corporate law and government counsel positions will be found in metropolitan areas where the possibilities are best for graduates of highly regarded schools and for those who graduate high in their classes.

Additional Source Material

Information Service
American Bar Association
1155 E. 60th Street
Chicago, IL 60637

Association of American Law Schools
Suite 370
1 Dupont Circle, N. W.
Washington, DC 20036

W. Curtis Brown

Buyer

W. Curtis Brown is a buyer for R. J. Reynolds Tobacco Company in Winston-Salem, North Carolina. He links outside salesmen and suppliers to Reynolds' engineering and manufacturing departments, and helps identify the suppliers offering best service, quality and price. He was selected for the job by Reynolds' personnel department. Previously, he was a junior engineer in the company's electric shop. He has a B.S. degree in electrical engineering from North Carolina Agricultural and Technical University (1958). He was born December 24, 1932 in Leighton, Alabama. His on-the-job training as a buyer included attending an American Management Association seminar, "Fundamentals of Purchasing for the Newly Appointed Buyer." He also participated in a buyer cross-training program to become familiar with other Reynolds buying assignments.

Mr. Brown estimates that less than 1 per cent of employees in the purchasing profession are black. He feels that "making blacks aware of the purchasing field and the important role it plays in a company's operation will generate interest and enthusiasm." He projects a 5 to 10 percent increase in the number of blacks in purchasing by 1978. He suggests that students interested in the field should acquaint themselves with marketing, manufacturing, finance and human elements of management.

Mr. Brown is a member of the Institute of Electrical and Electronics Engineers, Inc. He and his wife, Deloris, have two daughters, Delisa and Deidra. His leisure interests include sports, popular music and progressive jazz.

Career Information

Training
For beginning positions as buyers and purchasing agents, many employers prefer to hire graduates of schools of business administration or engineering who have had courses in accounting, economics and purchasing. On the other hand, many companies prefer experience within the firm and select purchasing employees from their own personnel. For advancement to high-level positions, however, a college education is becoming increasingly important. In any case, a new employee in purchasing must spend considerable time learning about that company's respective policies and purchasing procedures.

Outlook
For young people to enter and advance in the purchasing field, the prospects throughout this decade are good. Demand is anticipated for graduates of schools of business administration with purchasing backgrounds and for graduates having backgrounds in engineering and science for jobs in buying departments of firms that manufacture complex machinery, chemicals and other technical products.

Additional Source Material
American Marketing Association
230 North Michigan Ave.
Chicago, IL 60601

Patrick Hampton Butler
Corporation Counsel

Patrick Hampton Butler is an assistant cousel at Eli Lilly & Co. in Indianapolis, Indiana. He advises management on all federal and state laws and regulations affecting relations with employees. These include the Fair Labor Standards Act, all civil rights acts, the Occupational Safety and Health Act, the Labor Management and Disclosure Act, and wage control regulations. Eli Lilly & Co. is a major manufacturer of pharmaceuticals and agricultural products; its sales are more than $700 million a year.

Mr. Butler is a native of Gonzales, Texas. He has a B.A. degree (1956) from Colorado College and a J.D. degree (1961) from Colorado University School of Law. He feels that opportunities in his field will be good for blacks—"subject to a possible overpopulation of lawyers generally, resulting from increased enrollment in law schools." He and his wife, Barbara, have two children, Daphne and Ann. He is a golfer and is involved in various community activities in Indianapolis. He is a member of the American Bar Association.

Career Information

Training

There are many subfields within the general category of law. When people speak of engaging legal counsel they are referring to someone who has completed a minimum of three years of college work (although the number of lawyers without bachelor's degrees is infinitesimal) and who is a graduate of a law school approved by the American Bar Association or the proper state agencies. Furthermore, before a lawyer is allowed to practice in the court room, he must be admitted to the Bar of the state in which he intends to practice. As a rule, seven years of full-time study after high school are necessary to complete the requirements for a juris doctor (as the law degree is called). For students in prelegal studies, English, history, economics and other social sciences, logic and public speaking are important bases.

Outlook

Graduates from highly regarded law schools, as well as those who rank high in their classes, will have good employment prospects throughout the remainder of the decade. They should find opportunities for salaried positions with well-known law firms, on the legal staffs of corporations and government agencies, and as law clerks to judges. Graduates of the less prominent schools and those who graduate with lower scholastic ratings may experience some difficulty in finding salaried positions as lawyers. However, numerous opportunities will be available for law school graduates to enter a variety of other types of salaried positions requiring a knowledge of law.

Additional Source Material

Information Service
American Bar Association
1155 E. 60th Street
Chicago, Il 60637

Association of American Law Schools
Suite 370
1 Dupont Circle, NW
Washington, DC 20036

Dr. Hayward Campbell Jr.
Microbiologist

Dr. Hayward Campbell Jr., a microbiologist, is personnel director for science and medicine at Eli Lilly & Co. in Indianapolis, Indiana. He is responsible for all organizational development and personnel matters for the 2,000 persons in the firm's research, development, and control and medical research components. He was promoted to the position in 1973 after less than two years as managing director of Lilly Research Center, Ltd. in Windlesham, Surrey, England. Eli Lilly & Co. is a major manufacturer of pharmaceuticals, agricultural products and cosmetics; its 1971 sales were $723 million. Dr. Campbell has been with the firm since 1962.

Dr. Campbell, who was born April 30, 1934 in Abbeville, Louisiana, has a B.S. degree from Southern University in Louisiana and M.S. and Ph.D. degrees in microbiology from the University of Iowa. He believes that opportunities in his field are unlimited for blacks. He and his wife, Thomasine, have two daughters. He enjoys travel, golf and music.

Career Information

Training
Preparation for a career in microbiology must include college training—a minimum of a bachelor's degree for beginning positions in laboratories, etc. A master's degree or a doctorate is the general requirement for research positions or college or university teaching positions. Many schools in the United States offer degree programs in biology and its many subfields. Management responsibilities arise after experience on the job and are enhanced by appropriate training offered either within the company or through outside agencies.

Outlook
For those interested in microbiology, employment is expected to increase rapidly throughout the 1970s. However, along with the growing number of job openings, the number of life science graduates is also expected to increase rapidly. As a result, keen competition is anticipated for the more desirable positions. Opportunities for those holding only undergraduate degrees probably will be limited to positions as research assistant or technician.

Additional Source Material
American Institute of Biological Sciences
3900 Wisconsin Avenue, NW
Washington, DC 20016

Walter D. Chambers

Area Commercial Manager

Walter D. Chambers oversees fourteen district business offices for New Jersey Bell Telephone Company of East Orange, New Jersey. As area commercial manager, Mr. Chambers supervises the offices which handle collectively more than 350,000 telephone accounts in Essex County.

The responsibilities of Mr. Chambers' job also extend to coordination of community relations activities and those of the company's Affirmative Action Program. Before assuming his present position, Chambers was a personnel staff supervisor and a district managers. Although most of his training was obtained on the job, Mr. Chambers has a bachelor's degree in psychology from Lincoln University (1953) and a master's in human relations from New York University (1958).

Mr. Chambers estimates that future opportunities in his field will be excellent because, "The Bell System is committed to an Affirmative Action Program which guarantees opportunities based on individual qualifications."

40

Mr. Chambers is active in his community. He is chairman of the Newark Advisory Board of the Salvation Army and chairman of the public relations committee of the Robert Treat Council of the Boy Scouts of America. Born December 28, 1931 in Newark, New Jersey, he lives now in East Orange with his wife, Elizabeth and their two children, Keith and Courtney.

Career Information

Training
As with most managerial positions, a firm grounding in the specific company's operating procedures is required. Some firms promote experienced personnel from within the company, but in the coming decade, employers will be looking more to college graduates as management trainees. These graduates usually have a degree in business administration, personnel management or accounting. A masters in business administration, offered at an ever-growing number of colleges, universities and business schools, is particularly desirable for entry into lower level management jobs. On-the-job experience and continuing study determine promotion to top-level management jobs.

Outlook
New career opportunities for managers are expected to increase moderately through the 1970s; moreover, many vacancies will be created by normal occupational turnover. The employment of salaried managers is expected to increase rapidly because large firms tend to depend more on trained management specialists as companies grow in size.

Additional Source Material
The American Management Association
135 W. 50th Street
New York, NY 10020

Society for the Advancement of Management
1412 Broadway
New York, NY 10036

Jesse Clemons

Motel Manager

Jesse Clemons is innkeeper (general manager) of the Holiday Inn-River Bluff in Memphis, Tennessee. He was promoted after four years in such jobs as waiter, mâitre d' hôtel, assistant food and beverage manager, and director of management. To prepare further for his present position, he attended Holiday Inn University, the motel chain's training school.

Mr. Clemons has a B.S. degree in physical education from Tennessee Agricultural and Industrial State University. He believes that

future opportunities in hotel management are unlimited for blacks.

Mr. Clemons was born April 14, 1940 in Clarksdale, Mississippi. He and his wife, Mary, have no children. He is a member of Kappa Alpha Psi fraternity, the Hotel and Motel Association, and Brothers, Inc. He plays amateur football and golf.

Career Information

Training
Since most hotels promote from within, persons who have proven their ability, usually in front office jobs, may be promoted to assistant manager positions and eventually to general manager. Although hotel experience is generally the first consideration in selecting managers, employers are emphasizing a college education. Many believe that the best educational preparation is provided by colleges offering a specialized four-year curriculum in hotel and restaurant administration. Specialized courses in hotel work available at a few junior colleges, and study courses given by the Educational Institute of the American Hotel and Motel Association are also helpful. Some large hotel organizations have special programs for management trainees who are college graduates, or for less highly trained personnel promoted from within. These programs consist mainly of on-the-job training assignments in which the trainee is rotated among jobs in the various hotel departments. Some large hotels provide financial assistance to outstanding employees for college study.

Outlook
Well-qualified young people will find favorable opportunities to obtain entry positions that offer advancement possibilities for managerial work. Young applicants who have college degrees in hotel administration will have an advantage seeking entry positions and later advancement. Many openings for management personnel will result from normal occupational turnover.

Additional Source Material
American Hotel and Motel Association
888 7th Avenue
New York, NY 10019

Council on Hotel, Restaurant and Institutional Education
1522 K Street, NW
Washington, DC 20005

43

Lottie W. Cole

Medical Records Administrator

Lottie W. Cole is chief medical records administrator at Johns Hopkins Hospital in Baltimore, Maryland. With 170 people under her supervision, she has the responsibility of providing a system for acquiring, analyzing, sorting and retrieving a wide range of information—medical, statistical, socio-economic, etc. Her work is especially significant at a hospital such as Johns Hopkins which is, in addition to providing the usual patient care, deeply involved in research and education. Joining the hospital staff in 1951, she was supervisor of various sections of the large medical records department until she was appointed chief in 1965.

Born August 13, 1923 in Greensboro, N.C., Mrs. Cole has a B.A. degree from Shaw University. She did graduate work in history at Howard University and is a graduate of the U.S. Public Health Service Record Administration School. She was elected in 1970 to the executive board of the American Medical Record Association.

Of about four thousand registered record administrators in the country, Mrs. Cole estimates that fewer than one hundred are black. However, she feels that future opportunities are excellent. "Health-care professionals are very much in demand," she says.

In her spare time, Mrs. Cole enjoys swimming, jogging, roller skating and dancing. She also likes to sew; she makes many of her own clothes and those of her daughter. She is a member of United Methodist Women and the NAACP. She and her husband, James L., and their daughter, Brenda, live in Baltimore.

Career Information

Training
In 1970, twenty-eight schools located in colleges, universities and hospitals and approved by the American Medical Association offered training in medical record library science or medical record administration. The specialized curriculum includes both theoretical instruction and practical experience. The required courses included anatomy, physiology, fundamentals of medical science, medical terminology, medical record science, ethics, management, hospital organization and administration, health law, statistics and data processing. Graduates of approved schools in medical record science are eligible for the national registration examination given by the American Medical Record Association. Upon passing this examination, they receive professional recognition as Registered Record Librarians.

Outlook
Employment opportunities for graduates of approved medical record librarian programs are expected to be excellent in the 1970s.
High school graduates will have many opportunities to become medical record technicians to assist librarians (for information on medical record technicians and training programs for them, write to the address listed below).

Additional Source Material
The American Medical Record Association
875 North Michigan Avenue
Suite 1850
Chicago, Illinois 60611

Zeola H. Collins
Research Hematologist

Zeola H. Collins is manager of histocompatibility research for Hyland Laboratories, Costa Mesa, California. Histocompatibility deals with the matching of organ tissue, a very important phase of organ transplants. Hyland Laboratories is one of the first commercial firms to provide leukocyte (white blood cells) typing serums for organ transplantation.

Mrs. Collins directs five persons in the study of blood components toward developing products used in testing tissue compatibility. Before joining Hyland, Mrs. Collins worked in special hermatology at the City of Hope, a cancer research institution.

Born September 12, 1932, in St. Stephens, Alabama, Mrs. Collins received her bachelor's degree in 1953 from Alabama State College. She is an avid baseball fan and her ambition is to find time to manage a Little League team. Mrs. Collins and her husband Alonzo have three children.

Career Information

Training

Beginning positions dealing with tissue preparation (histology) and blood analysis (hematology) are prepared for with four years of post high school training. This would include completion of a specialized training program in medical technology approved by the American Medical Association. Undergraduate work must include courses in chemistry, biology and mathematics. The additional specialized education usually requires a year of study and extensive laboratory work. Many universities offer advanced degrees in medical technology and related subjects for technologists who plan to specialize in the laboratory or in teaching, administration or research.

Outlook

Employment opportunities for medical laboratory workers of all types are expected to be excellent through the 1970s. New graduates having a bachelor's degree will be sought for entry positions in hospitals. A particularly strong demand is anticipated for technologists having graduate training in biochemistry, microbiology, immunology and virology.

Additional Source Material

Registry of Medical Technologists of the
American Society of Clinical Pathologists
710 South Wolcott Avenue
Chicago, IL 60612

American Society of Medical Technologists
Suite 1600, Hermann Professional Building
Houston, TX 77025

American Medical Technologists
710 Higgins Road
Park Ridge, IL 60068

Colonel Hannibal M. Cox Jr.

Airline Ground Support Director

Hannibal M. Cox Jr., a retired United States Air Force colonel, is director of ground support equipment for Eastern Airlines in Miami, Florida. He has system-wide responsibility for buying, distributing and maintaining all such equipment for the airline. There are ninety-five persons on his staff.

Colonel Cox obtained his position, a newly created one at Eastern, through an EAL officer he met while in the air force. Born March 21, 1923 in Chicago, Illinois, he has a B.S. degree in aeronautics from Tennessee State University, an M.B.A. in industrial relations and personnel management from the University of Chicago, and a degree in personnel services from George Peabody College in Nashville,

48

Tennessee. He has also completed requirements for a Ph.D. degree in psychology at West Colorado University. Colonel Cox was a member of the 99th Fighter Squadron during World War II, and is the only black pilot to have flown fighter planes in World War II, the Korean War, and the Vietnam War. He feels that opportunities in maintenance and engineering are unlimited for blacks. Colonel Cox and his wife, Margaret, live in Miami. He has a son, Michael, a daughter, Michelle, and two stepchildren, Julienne and Michael. He lists golf, power boating and writing among his leisure interests. He is a member of the American Management Association, the Air Force Association and Kappa Alpha Psi fraternity.

Career Information

Training
For a position dealing with aircraft and its support equipment, a degree in engineering is desirable. A degree program in aerospace engineering is especially good background. In positions requiring purchasing, such as ground support director, all the purchasing requisites should be filled. These include a degree in business administration or management.

Outlook
Continuing developments in supersonic, subsonic and vertical lift aircraft, and advancement in space and missile activities, should result in a moderate increase in the need for aerospace engineers. However, engineers who are not well grounded in engineering fundamentals and those whose specialization is very narrow could be affected by skill obsolescence caused by shifts in defense activities and by rapidly changing technology.

Additional Source Material
American Institute of Aeronautics and Astronautics, Inc.
1290 Avenue of the Americas
New York, NY 10019

Annie V. Davis

Administrative Associate, Test Scheduling

Annie V. Davis is an administrative associate at the New York (N.Y.) Testing Center of Avon Products, Inc., a cosmetics manufacturing and distributing company. She schedules test projects and test panelists into the center, where Avon products undergo quality examinations. She also evaluates results, drafts final reports and develops new evaluation systems. She has developed a numerical

system that makes it possible to pinpoint with high accuracy certain performance features of Avon products. She was a product development chemist with Avon before she was promoted.

Born September 21, 1934 in Ithaca, New York, Miss Davis has a B.S. degree in chemistry from Cornell University. Because of the growth of ethnic (particularly black) markets, Miss Davis feels there is a great need for more blacks to enter her field. Opportunities should be great in the future, she believes.

In her leisure time, Miss Davis designs and makes her own clothes, and reads and writes science fiction.

Career Information

Training
There is no prescribed educational course to follow for a position as an administrative associate. Promotion to such a supervisory post comes usually after much grounding in a specific company's operating procedures. For those interested in entry at the management level, training is discussed under other management occupations. Generally, however, employees seeking promotion enhance their possibilities by taking advantage of numerous programs offered through local institutions and correspondence courses, and sometimes at the place of employment.

Outlook
The outlook for the rest of the decade for managerial positions is very good as large corporations seek the expertise of specialized managers. Promotion from within the ranks is very possible in technical jobs where a thorough understanding of industrial processes is required. For entry-level positions and management trainees, those with a college background have the greatest prospects.

Additional Source Material
The American Management Association
135 W. 50th Street
New York, NY 10020

Society for Advancement of Management
1412 Broadway
New York, NY 10036

William Dilday

Television Station Manager

William Dilday manages WLBT-TV in Jackson, Mississippi, the first black station manager in the nation. His responsibilities cover the entire range of the station's operations, including supervision of promotion and programming managers.

Prior to his appointment to WLBT in a racially prompted management reshuffling, Mr. Dilday was personnel director for television station WHDH in Boston, Massachusetts. He has a degree from the Boston University School of Business.

The example set by Mr. Dilday, that is, restaffing WLBT to employ 30 percent blacks, is "something all the stations in this country are going to have to do," he says. For those who lacked adequate experience, Mr. Dilday has provided on-the-job training.

Born September 14, 1937, in Boston, Mr. Dilday is married and the father of two daughters. In spite of the fact that the Dildays had not been farther south than Washington, D.C. before his appointment, they are convinced that they will stay in the South. Mr. Dilday spends his leisure time with his family.

Career Information

Training
In the case of television, managers are generally promoted from the ranks of experienced personnel. Those who eventually rise to station manager responsibility were, in some cases, program managers, news or promotion directors. Training for positions at entry-level may be through degree programs offered at an increasing number of colleges, universities and communications schools. Management training is also an excellent entry-level background (see *Training* under other management occupations).

Outlook
While those seeking entrance into radio and television careers are going to face stiff competition throughout the seventies, opportunities for blacks should be somewhat better because of new hiring guidelines.

Additional Source Material
For information on the managerial aspects of television write to:

The American Management Association
135 W. 50th Street
New York, NY 10020

Society for the Advancement of Management
1412 Broadway
New York, NY 10036

John M. Dixon

Director of Hotel Sales Coordination

John M. Dixon is employed as the director of sales coordination—Inns Division—for ITT Sheraton Hotels and Motels in Boston, Massachusetts. Mr. Dixon acts as the liaison between the Inns Division and the corporate sales staff. He also creates and implements programs for the black, aged and youth special markets in addition to doing sales training for the corporation. He was referred to Sheraton by an executive search firm. He has a bachelor's degree from the University of Montana and a law degree from the New England School of Law. He is a member of the Inter-American Travel Agents and the National Association of Market Developers. Most of his free time is spent working for a master's degree in business administration. Mr. Dixon was born January 25, 1938 in Chicago, Illinois. He and his wife, Rosalie, have a son, Kwame Dubois.

Career Information

Training
Within the fields of sales and marketing, there are countless subfields, most of which require similar educational backgrounds at the entry level with specialization coming after some experience with a company, and a firm grounding in that company's operating procedures. The salesman who sells complex products or services (or whose selling procedures are complicated by the highly technical nature of the manufacturing process) may sometimes receive training that lasts for months. For some positions, salesmen must be college graduates who have majored in engineering or some other field. Still others gain experience through years of on-the-job training. A director of sales coordination with responsibility for special markets must have skills in market analysis. In cases where the position involves training of other personnel, the coordinator must have complete knowledge of the company's sales procedures, policies and marketing goals. The only way to prepare for such a specialization is with the particular company, but for those who intend to enter at the management level, a college degree in marketing or related fields is invaluable.

Outlook
New career opportunities for managers are expected to increase moderately. Large firms tend to rely more heavily on trained management specialists as their size increases and problems in communications and industrial complexity require a higher ratio of managers to other employes.

Additional Source Material
The American Management Association
135 W. 50th Street
New York, NY 10020

Sales and Marketing Executives International
Student Education Division
630 Third Avenue
New York, NY 10017

Kenneth Easter

Industrial Sales Engineer

Kenneth Easter is an industrial sales engineer for the Timken Roller Bearing Company of Canton, Ohio. His job requires that he be qualified to assist manufacturers in all engineering aspects where roller bearings are required.

Mr. Easter joined Timken from Goodyear Aerospace Corporation where he was a recovery systems development engineer. He holds a bachelor's degree in aerospace engineering from Indiana Institute of Technology and is currently attending Akron University School of Law.

Born August 16, 1944, in Pittsburgh, Pennsylvania, Mr. Easter was awarded a U. S. patent in 1968 for the design of a two-stage decelerator for re-entry into the earth's atmosphere.

Married and the father of two children, Mr. Easter attends classes in small business training and operation given by the Small Business Administration. His leisure activities include listening to music, and participating in sports.

56

Career Information

Training

The required training for a position as an industrial sales engineer is fairly rigorous. The preferred degree is one in mechanical engineering, courses for which give a firm grounding in mechanical applications and the production and use of power. The newly hired engineer often undergoes a lengthy training period during which his or her theoretical training is applied to the specific production practices of the company. Generally speaking, then, the student interested in industrial sales should prepare with a degree in mechanical engineering available at some 270 colleges and universities in the United States. The first two years of the four-year curriculum are devoted to mathematics, physics and chemistry; the last two are devoted to a specialty (in this case, mechanical applications).

Outlook

The prospects for employment in engineering are best for those with a mechanical specialty. The expected expansion of industry with the consequent demand for industrial machinery and machine tools, and the increasing technological complexity of machinery and processes will be among the major factors contributing to greater employment. Additional spaces will be created by normal occupational turnover.

Additional Source Material

The American Society of Mechanical
   Engineers
345 E. 47th Street
New York, NY 10017

George R. Edwards
Franchise Development Director

George R. Edwards is director of franchise development at Pepsico International in Purchase, New York. He develops marketing plans for franchise bottlers around the world. He was promoted after eight and one-half years as a general sales manager, a marketing planning manager and a salesman. Before coming to Pepsico, bottlers of the soft drink Pepsi Cola, he worked for seven years in the marketing and sales departments of an international airline. He has a B.A. degree in education from the City College of New York. "Marketing as a careeer opportunity has offered many blacks a number of positions within its framework," he says, "but blacks in international marketing still appear to be very scarce." He adds that opportunities will increase as more blacks with experience and better training enter major corporations.

Mr. Edwards was born February 1, 1938 in Grenada, West Indies. He and his wife, Patsy, have two children, Lisa and George. They live in Danbury, Connecticut. He is a member of the American Marketing Association. In his spare time, he enjoys basketball, swimming and music.

Career Information

Training

For those involved in any kind of market development, the requisite skills are many. The developer must be able to appraise market situations and plan market policies. The general theoretical bases for these skills are available only through college courses in marketing, finance, statistics and related fields. The all-important knowledge of a particular company's policies and procedures is available only at that company and can be attained through internal training institutes.

Outlook

The demand for marketing services encompassed within the development field is expected to increase very rapidly throughout the 1970s. As more and more companies open branches (especially international subsidiaries), employers will find it necessary to turn to specialists in development areas.

Additional Source Material

American Marketing Association
230 North Michigan Avenue
Chicago, IL 60601

Sales and Marketing Executives International
Student Education Division
630 Third Avenue
New York, NY 10017

James E. Farmer
Budget Manager

James E. Farmer is manager of budget administration at the Airtemp Division of the Chrysler Corporation in Dayton, Ohio. Airtemp manufactures air conditioning and heating equipment. Mr. Farmer is responsible for developing and preparing all marketing department budgets, including those for advertising and sales promotion. Promoted to his position in 1971 by the vice president of marketing, he previously

was advertising coordinator and government sales coordinator. He joined Airtemp shortly after graduating in 1967 from Central State University, where he obtained a B.S. degree in marketing and took courses in data processing. He also took graduate courses at the University of Dayton. He is a scroller of Kappa Alpha Psi fraternity and is a member of the American Marketing Association and the Society for the Advancement of Management.

Although, according to Mr. Farmer, it is still somewhat rare for a black man to occupy a position like his, he feels that the field is opening because of the increased emphasis on marketing rather than strictly on business administration.

Active in community affairs such as the United Appeal Committee, he is especially involved with young people and serves as adviser to the Dayton branch of Junior Achievement, a national organization which encourages young people in business. For relaxation, Mr. Farmer enjoys reading, skating and bowling. Born August 8, 1945 in Dayton, he is single.

Career Information

Training
Managerial positions come in differentiated levels—entry, middle-level, and top. Before rising to the latter two, time is spent either as a supervisor or management trainee. Employers increasingly require beginning managers to have completed college. Although a person who doesn't have a degree may rise through the ranks, promotional opportunities are becoming limited. Many employers look for persons with a college degree in business administration, with a major in accounting, economics or finance. Others look for persons with technical training, while others hire liberal arts graduates and train them on the job.

Outlook
Possible slots for managers are expected to increase moderately through the 1970s. Additionally, many thousands of openings are likely to occur because of occupational turnover.

Additional Source Material
The American Management Association
135 W. 50th Street
New York, NY 10020

Society for Advancement of Management
1412 Broadway
New York, NY 10036

Sandra D. Farrington
Physician's Associate

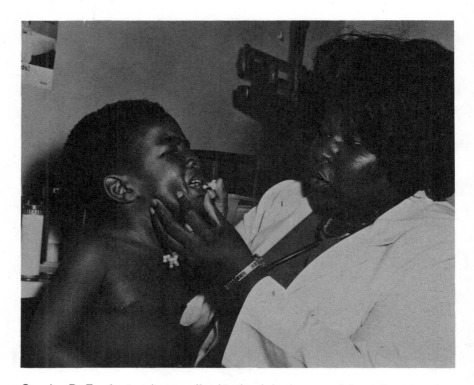

Sandra D. Farrington is a pediatric physician's associate at the Lincoln Community Health Center in Durham, North Carolina. A little over four years ago, Mrs. Farrington went on welfare but constantly sought other means to support her children. She was referred to the Durham New Careers program, one of many around the country financed by the United States Department of Labor.

Through New Careers, she enrolled in a course for operating room technicians at the University of North Carolina. There her work was so good that she was recommended for the physician's associate program at Duke University. In spite of the heavy workload and long course of training, Mrs. Farrington received her diploma as a physician's associate, a new position in hospitals designed to free doctors of the more routine medical responsibilities.

As a physician's associate, Mrs. Farrington takes patient histories, conducts physical examinations and orders laboratory work where necessary. Her pre-screening aids the doctor in diagnosing and prescribing treatment for the patients.

Mrs. Farrington gets particular satisfaction from working with infants, children and adolescents. "It makes me really happy to work with youngsters from the same background I came from," she says, and hopes that she will provide an encouraging model.

Divorced and the mother of five children, Mrs. Farrington has little free time, but she does enjoy bowling, listening to music and dancing. Born on March 15, 1940, in Durham, N.C., she and her children live in Durham.

Career Information

Training

Physician's associates train for their positions through special programs established at university schools of medicine. The field is very new and is offered at a limited number of schools at the time of this writing. Generally speaking, those studying for a diploma take two years of classroom and clinic training. Courses studied include anatomy, physiology, chemistry, biology, pharmacology and clinical diagnosis. Acceptance in the program depends on the applicant's background, for many of the trainees in the physician's associate programs are registered nurses or former Armed Forces medical corpsmen. At least a high school education and some medical study (such as that available at vocational-technical schools, junior and community colleges) beyond that is a good background.

Outlook

The outlook for physician's associates and other health-related occupations is very good throughout the seventies. With the pressure on hospitals to provide more comprehensive care and the additional staff requirements of clinics, the demand is expected to rise rapidly.

Additional Source Material

Contact the state employment office for information on programs offered through the Manpower Development Training Act. Or write to:
American Association of Medical Assistants
200 East Ohio Street
Chicago, IL 60611

Hughlyn F. Fierce

Commercial Loan Officer

Hughlyn F. Fierce is a vice president and commercial loan officer at Chase Manhattan Bank in New York, New York. He graduated from Morgan State College with a B.A. degree in economics and from New York University with an M.B.A. degree in finance. He participated in Chase Manhattan's special development program and worked for a while in the credit department. He estimates that no more than fifty

black commercial loan officers work in major U.S. banks, but believes opportunities will be increasingly good. Mr. Fierce and his wife, Jewel, live in Brooklyn, New York. They have three children. In his spare time, Mr. Fierce works with the Interracial Council for Business Opportunities and the United Cerebral Palsy National Association.

Career Information

Training
Bank officer positions may be filled by management trainees or by promoting experienced clerical employees. A business administration major in finance or a liberal arts curriculum including accounting, economics, commercial law, political science and statistics serves as excellent preparation for entry-level training programs. A master's degree in business administration greatly enhances employment possibilities.

Outlook
The number of such bank officers is expected to increase rapidly as banking activities expand. Many openings for college graduates will be made by normal occupational turnover. Although college graduates who meet the standards for executive trainees should find good opportunities, many appointments as officers will arise from experienced employees within the bank. Competition for these promotions will be keen, especially among the larger banks.

Additional Source Material
American Bankers Association
Personnel Administration and Manpower Development Committee
1120 Connecticut Avenue, NW
Washington, DC 20036

National Association of Bank Women, Inc.
National Office
111 E. Wacker Drive
Chicago, IL 60601

National Bankers Association
4310 Georgia Avenue, NW
Washington, DC 20011

Delbert Flowers

Industrial Hygienist

Delbert L. Flowers serves as an industrial hygienist with the Occupational Safety and Health Administration, U.S. Department of Labor in Washington, D. C. It is his responsibility to recognize, evaluate and control occupational health hazards found in various types of working environments. When hazardous conditions arise from dust, vapors, gases, noise, radiation or the use of chemicals, Mr. Flowers recommends measures for protecting workers.

Mr. Flowers has a bachelor's degree in biology and chemistry, and earned his master of science degree in industrial hygiene from the University of Michigan at Ann Arbor. He began as an industrial hygiene technician and has since developed on-site hygiene programs for several companies. Mr. Flowers joined the OSHA from the IBM Corporation, where he initiated and implemented a comprehensive industrial hygiene and air pollution program for two manufacturing facilities and one research laboratory.

According to Mr. Flowers, there are unlimited opportunities for blacks in the field of industrial hygiene. He was himself instrumental in the development of the Target Health Hazards Program for isolating exposures to silica, asbestos, lead, cotton dust and carbon monoxide among United States workers, many of whom are black.

Born on October 22, 1930 in Hamilton, Ohio, Mr. Flowers lives with his wife Pearl and their three children in Rockville, Maryland. He enjoys

golf and photography, working in the community and participating in Kappa Alpha Psi Fraternity activities.

Career Information

Training
Most degrees for industrial hygiene are offered at the graduate level. Those seeking entry-level positions should have a bachelor's degree in a science with a concentration in chemistry, biology or, in some cases, engineering. Most beginning employees enter at the technician level, and educational preparation for engineering and science technicians can be obtained from a wide variety of institutions—from the vocational-technical high school to the four-year college. Advancement comes after on-the-job experience or further specialized training. As of this writing, there are a few four-year institutions which offer a degree in industrial hygiene (or occupational health and safety). Many schools, however, have degree programs in the sciences for that all-important training that eases entrance possibilities.

Outlook
The outlook for the rest of the decade is expected to be very good. The demand will be strongest for graduates of post-secondary school technician-training programs. The growing intricacy of the production process, continued expenditures in research and development and the growth of new technical areas all contribute to the call for more engineering and science technicians. Also, positions will be created by normal occupational turnover.

Additional Source Material
American Society for Engineering Education
Suite 400
1 Dupont Circle
Washington, DC 20036

Engineers' Council for Professional
  Development
345 E. 47th Street
New York, NY 10017

National Council of Technical Schools
1835 K Street, NW
Room 907
Washington, DC 20006

Adrienne Frye
Construction Office Manager

Adrienne Frye is site office manager for Paschen Contractors, Inc., Chicago, Illinois. Working at construction sites, including one for a new federal building in the Loop business district, Mrs. Frye purchases construction equipment and supplies, approves payments to suppliers and subcontractors, handles payrolls for workers and makes reports to the building owners.

Mrs. Frye gained her knowledge of construction work while a secretary with the firm, where she had an opportunity to familiarize herself with trade terms and equipment. On the basis of this knowledge, she was promoted to her present position, an unusual one for a woman. Mrs. Frye was a music and business administration major at Wilson Jr. College in Chicago.

Born May 2, 1931 in Chicago, Mrs. Frye is the mother of three children: Nathan, Jacqueline and Kevin. In her leisure moments, she enjoys the theater.

Career Information

Training
While not demanding a college education, the management of a construction office requires a knowledge of technical language, equipment specifications, some labor law, business mathematics and familiarity with government regulations affecting the trade. A high school business background helps for entry into a clerical or on-site position that could lead to office management after some experience in the field. As with all managerial positions, however, a college degree in business administration is the best qualification for high-level entry.

Outlook
Even though employment in the construction industry is likely to grow, the increasing application of the latest technology in tools, material and work methods, together with the rising skill level of the work force, will make it possible to increase the level of construction activity without a correspondingly large increase in employment. Concomitantly, qualifications for employment are expected to rise rapidly. Therefore, adequate preparation is necessary.

Additional Source Material
AFL-CIO
Building and Construction Trades Department
815 16th Street, NW
Washington, DC 20006

Associated General Contractors of America, Inc.
1957 E Street, NW
Washington, DC 20006

National Association of Home Builders
1625 L Street, NW
Washington, DC 20036

Gene Ann Furman
Computer Specialist

Gene Ann Furman is a computer specialist employed by Joseph E. Seagram & Sons, Inc. in New York, New York. She writes instructions for processing various types of information into computer language. Prior to attaining her present position, Miss Furman worked for four summers at Seagram as a receptionist, typist, clerk and secretary. She has a B.S. degree (1968) in

psychology from Vassar College and studied at the Honeywell Electronic Data Processing School. She also has had on-the-job training and has taken IBM systems courses. Miss Furman feels that although there are many black keypunch and computer operators, there are relatively too few programmers. She believes that, with increasing computerization, there will be many opportunities in her field for blacks. Miss Furman was born March, 19, 1946 in Louisville, Kentucky. She is single and enjoys tennis, travel, handicrafts, music and reading.

Career Information

Training
Young people interested in programming can acquire some of the necessary skills at a steadily growing number of technical schools, colleges and universities. The special abilities most sought by employers when they hire programmers are similar to those for almost all other types of positions, but requirements regarding education and experience vary according to the problems with which the programmer will be occupied. For almost all positions, an applicant who has no college training is at a severe disadvantage. Additionally, on-the-job training is required.

Outlook
Many thousands of new jobs for programmers will become available each year through the 1970s. The increase in employment is expected to be particularly sharp in firms that use computers to process records or to control manufacturing processes.

Additional Source Material
Data Processing Management Association
505 Busse Highway
Park Ridge, IL 60068

American Federation of Information
Processing Societies
210 Summit Avenue
Montvale, NJ 07645

Frank Edward Gainer

Assay Coordinator

Frank Edward Gainer is an antibiotic assay coordinator at Eli Lilly and Co. in Indianapolis, Indiana. He supervises and coordinates a department (of forty-two persons) responsible for analyzing company-produced antibiotics and links operations of his department with other operations in the company's antibiotic producing facilities.

An employee of Eli Lilly since 1967, Dr. Gainer was a senior analytical chemist before he was promoted in 1972. He is a graduate of Morehouse College (B.S., chemistry, 1960), Tuskegee Institute (M.S., chemistry, 1962) and Iowa State University of Science and Technology (M.S., analytical chemistry, 1964; Ph.D., analytical chemistry, 1967). He is a member of the American Chemical Society.

Blacks in a job like his are rare, Dr. Gainer says, probably because relatively few blacks have background in analytical chemistry. "Future opportunities, however, are good," he believes. "Fortunately, analytical chemists are still in demand by industry even though there have been cutbacks in other disciplines in recent years." He adds that analytical chemists "can easily adapt to interdisciplinary kinds of job settings such as clinical chemistry, drug abuse studies, pollution and ecology, oceanography, geology, and space exploration."

Dr. Gainer was bron June 18, 1938 in Waynesboro, Georgia. He and his wife, Alvie, have two sons, Edward and Ervin. In his spare time he enjoys table tennis, shuffleboard, bowling and traveling.

Career Information

Training

Chemistry is a flexible field in which the analytical chemist can adapt his training to clinical chemistry, drug abuse studies, pollution and ecology, oceanography, geology and space exploration. Graduates holding only a bachelor's degree in chemistry usually begin their careers in industry or government working in applied research. Often, special training programs designed to supplement college training and determine the new entrants' area of specialization are offered by industry and government. Those with interest in research or college teaching must have a graduate (doctorate) degree.

Outlook

The employment outlook for chemists is expected to continue at a favorable level through the seventies. New opportunities will be supplied by rapid growth of research and development and vacancies created by normal occupational turnover.

Additional Source Material

American Chemical Society
1155 16th Street, N W
Washington, DC 20036

Manufacturing Chemists' Association
1825 Connecticut Avenue, N W
Washington, DC 20009

Constance O'Neil Garretson

Sales Promotion Specialist

Constance O'Neil Garretson is a sales promotion specialist at
Prudential Insurance Company of America in Newark, New Jersey. She
and her staff of five create sales aids and provide sales and promotional
ideas for individual life and health insurance plans. She directs the
planning and development of material for sales campaigns, and acts as
a consultant for other departments and representatives throughout the
United States, Germany and Puerto Rico. She has held numerous jobs
in her twenty-one years with Prudential, and obtained her present
position through promotion from assistant sales promotion specialist. A
graduate of Howard University in English, she has taken life insurance
office management association courses. "Blacks in middle management
in a creative area are very rare in any life insurance corporate home
office," she says. "Female blacks in such positions are even more
rare." Future opportunities for blacks in sales promotion, she believes
to be unlimited. Mrs. Garretson is the first black woman to be
designated by the American College of Life Underwriters as a Chartered
Life Underwriter, and said she may be the "only black woman holding
a job which has such a large part in influencing the sales of one
of the giants of American industry."

She is vice president of Friends of the Newark Community Center of the Arts, an organization formed to develop in youth an appreciation for the performing arts. She is also a member of Black Expression in Art, which presents qualified black artists to the public. A member of the Women's Political Caucus, she has visited twenty-six countries, and toured the United States, including Hawaii. Mrs. Garretson lives in East Orange, New Jersey.

Career Information

Training

Unfortunately, there are no uniformly agreed upon requirements for entry into sales positions. In most cases, those interested in sales on the management level must have a college degree in marketing, finance, business administration or a related field. This is for *entry* on the management level. It is not impossible to rise to a management position through experience with a company; indeed, even those with college training must undergo orientation into a specific company's marketing goals and procedures. A sales promotion specialist (who creates sales aids and promotional ideas) must have a thorough familiarity with the product or service, must have training in market analysis methods and must have creative ability in order to guide the design of attractive promotions. Many large companies offer training institutes, or courses in marketing techniques are available through private organizations and local colleges or universities.

Outlook

While the outlook for the employment of sales and marketing specialists is quite favorable throughout the seventies, prospects are best for those with good theoretical bases provided by specialized college training. Market complexities and increased data accumulation demands that employers seek people with the basic requisite skills and the need for only minor additional training.

Additional Source Material

American Marketing Association
230 North Michigan Avenue
Chicago, IL 60601

Sales and Marketing Executives International
Student Education Division
630 Third Avenue
New York, NY 10017

Marcus G. Gibson

Transit Superintendent

Marcus Garvey Gibson is employed by the New York City Transit
Authority in New York, New York as assistant general superintendent
for surface transit. He is responsible for policies affecting all surface
routes and scheduled service budgets, construction, engineering and
labor relations. He prepares the operating and capital budgets and is
responsible for the maintenance of buildings and grounds. More than
five thousand surface operators (bus drivers, etc.) and nearly
six hundred supervisory personnel come under his authority.

76

Mr. Gibson, who was born May 22, 1922 in Brooklyn, New York, began work at the Transit Authority in 1942 as a bus repairman. He passed successive civil service examinations, moving up through the ranks over a 27-year period before attaining his present position in 1969. He has attended management and transportation seminars at New York and Pennsylvania State universities and the University of Pittsburgh. He and his wife, Bernice, have two sons, Michael and Gary, and a daughter, Karen. He enjoys hunting, bowling and fishing.

Career Information

Training
Beginning positions that lead to supervision in the transit field are prepared for by earning a bachelor's degree in transportation from any of the several schools in the United States that offer them. A curriculum which includes courses in management is particularly good preparation. It is possible for an employee to work his or her way up through the ranks on the basis of on-the-job experience, but for entry at the low management level, a college degree is required. For those without a college degree, advancement possibilities are enhanced by taking part in transit management seminars and other courses in management offered by company institutes and local colleges and universities.

Outlook
Generally speaking, opportunities in management are expected to be favorable throughout the remainder of the decade. As described above, employers are increasingly seeking those with a college education as management trainees.

Additional Source Material
The American Management Association
135 W. 50th Street
New York, NY 10020

Society for Advancement of Management
1412 Broadway
New York, NY 10036

William W. Gore
Traffic Assistant

William W. Gore is traffic assistant at R. J. Reynolds Tobacco Company in Winston-Salem, North Carolina. His work involves distribution of manufactured tobacco products from factories to public warehouses and finally to customers. He handles correspondence with warehouses, transportation companies and customers as it relates to distribution of Reynolds products in various territories. He also prepares distribution cost studies for transportation and storage of products.

Blacks are rare in the industrial traffic area of transportation and distribution, but Mr. Gore believes that "the opportunities are very widespread, ranging from positions with industry to related positions with airlines, railroads, trucking companies and steamship lines." Mr. Gore was born May 1, 1942 in Bolivia, North Carolina. He has a B.S. degree from North Carolina Agricultural and Technical State University. He is a member of Delta Nu Alpha transportation fraternity, and the American Society of Traffic and Transportation. He and his wife, Elnora, have a son, Michael Anthony. Mr. Gore's interests include music, reading, sports, travel and photography.

Career Information

Training
Although a person having only a high school education can qualify for a traffic manager position on the basis of experience in a traffic department, (as a traffic assistant, etc.) a college education is becoming increasingly important for a career in this field. Some employers prefer a graduate having a degree in traffic management. Such a degree is available at more than 100 universities, colleges and junior colleges. Other employers prefer liberal arts majors who have had courses in transportation, management, economics, statistics, marketing or commercial law.

Outlook
A moderate increase in employment in this occupation is expected throughout the 1970s. Many new industrial traffic manager positions will be created as corporations reorganize their shipping and receiving activities into separate traffic departments to centrally control their transportation functions.

Additional Source Material
American Society of Traffic and Transportation, Inc.
22 W. Madison Street
Chicago, IL 60602

Lester L. Hale

Advertising Account Manager

Lester L. Hale is account manager-advertising at Hart, Schaffner & Marx in Chicago, Illinois. He is the clothing manufacturer's in-house advertising account manager. His work includes serving as liaison between management advertising objectives and the company's advertising department.

Mr. Hale joined HS&M as a management trainee. He has a B.S. degree in marketing from Southern Illinois University and an M.B.A. degree in finance and accounting from Northwestern University. He was born December 9, 1948 in Aberdeen, Mississippi.

His job is unique, Mr. Hale believes, in that few blacks have had the training to accommodate a management position in advertising. He feels that future opportunities for blacks are immense.

Mr. Hale is a sportsman in his spare time.

Career Information

Training
Most employers, in hiring advertising trainees, prefer college graduates having liberal arts training or majors in advertising, marketing, journalism or business administration. However, there is no typical educational background for success in advertising. Young people planning to enter the field should get some experience in copywriting or related work with their school publications and, if possible, through summer jobs connected with marketing research services. Some large advertising organizations recruit outstanding college graduates and train them in all aspects of advertising work. Most beginners, however, have to locate their own jobs by applying directly to agencies. For entrance on a management level, the applicant should have the requisite skills as described elsewhere under other managerial occupations.

Outlook
Employment of advertising workers is expected to increase only slowly through the 1970s. Opportunities should be favorable, however, for highly qualified applicants, especially in agencies, as more and more companies turn their work over to outside firms to handle. However, many young people interested in advertising will face stiff competition for entry jobs in this field through the 1970s. Most openings result from occupational fluctuations.

Additional Source Material
American Advertising Federation
1225 Connecticut Avenue, NW
Washington, DC 20036

American Association of Advertising Agencies
200 Park Avenue
New York, NY 10017

Association of Industrial Advertisers
41 E. 42nd Street
New York, NY 10017

Donald C. Haley

Tax Accountant

Donald C. Haley manages the tax and corporate accounting department at Standard Oil Company (Ohio) in Cleveland, Ohio. He is responsible for the overall corporate tax compliance, planning and tax audit activities, corporate financial consolidations, forecasting and budgeting, and preparation of financial statements. Previously, he was a tax attorney in the company's corporate legal department. He has a B.S. degree in accounting from the University of Illinois (1950), an M.B.A. degree from Western Reserve University (1958) and a J.D. degree from Cleveland-Marshall Law School (1963). He is a certified public accountant. In 1970, he was admitted to practice before the U.S. Tax Court.

According to Mr. Haley, there are very few blacks engaged in tax or corporate accounting work. Thus, because the demand for qualified people is so great, "it is a field of unrestricted opportunity." He believes that blacks should "seek out positions of authority and influence in both the public and private sector of our society." He says: "The benefits are clear. We can exert direct influence in hiring, firing and promotion. We have the opportunity to influence a greater concern and commitment of the decision-makers toward our collective advancement, and we can learn the techniques employed in successful business operations."

Mr. Haley was born March 15, 1928 in Peoria, Illinois. He and his wife, Janice, have three sons: Randle, Gordon and Steven. He enjoys golf, general outdoor activities, travel and community activities.

Career Information

Training

Training in accounting can be obtained in universities, colleges, junior colleges, accounting and private business schools and through correspondence courses. Graduates of all these institutions are included in the ranks of successful accountants. However, a bachelor's degree with a major in accounting or a closely related field is increasingly an asset. For better positions, it may be required. Candidates having a master's degree in accounting, as well as college training in other business and liberal arts subjects, are preferred by many firms. Since accountants often specialize in such areas as auditing, taxes, cost accounting, budgeting and control, information processing or systems and procedures, the accounting student should pick his area of specialization and structure the college curriculum around it.

Outlook

Accounting employment is expected to expand very rapidly during the 1970s because of greater use of accounting information in business management, complex and changing tax systems, the growth in size and number of corporations required to provide financial reports to stockholders, and the increasing use of accounting services by small business organizations. As a result, opportunities for accountants are expected to be excellent.

Additional Source Material

National Association of Accountants
505 Park Avenue
New York, NY 10022

National Society of Public Accountants
1717 Pennsylvania Avenue, NW
Washington, DC 20006

Financial Executives Institute
50 W. 44th Street
New York, NY 10036

The Institute of Internal Auditors, Inc.
170 Broadway
New York, NY 10038

James L. Hall
Chief of Plant Security

James L. Hall is chief of plant security at the Chevrolet Saginaw Manufacturing Plant in Saginaw, Michigan. He supervises the thirty-man security and fire protection force at the plant, where some two thousand employees produce front disc brakes for most General Motors automobiles and trucks. He is the first black person in such a position at a General Motors Corporation facility.

Born October 31, 1936 in Saginaw, Mr. Hall attended Bay City Community College (he studied radio-television communications) and Saginaw Valley Community College (for studies in psychology and sociology). He and his wife, Carole, have four daughters: Jebene, Lynn, Jennifer and Kellie.

Career Information

Training

Industrial plants have found the need to engage in large security operations as plants have grown in size and complexity. Plant security networks employ many men and often the latest detection and communication equipment to link areas of the plant and its grounds. A supervisor of such a force may be promoted from within the ranks, or may join a company after specialized training in management and undergo additional training and orientation for that particular company's operating procedures. The best educational background to offer when applying for such a position is a degree in industrial management (see *Training* under other management occupations).

Outlook

Because of the growing need for security forces among larger industries, employment prospects can be expected to be good in the future. Management slots are likely to open up as these firms institute broad security where small forces existed previously.

Additional Source Material

American Management Association
135 W. 50th Street
New York, NY 10020

Robert D. Harris
Labor Relations Manager

Robert D. Harris is manager of labor relations (Akron Plants) at Firestone Tire and Rubber Company in Akron, Ohio. He negotiates collective bargaining agreements with unions for six plants, serves as chief company spokesman for grievances and handles day-to-day labor problems. He has a B.A. degree in political science (1966) from West Virginia State College, and completed Firestone's college class training program in industrial relations and its advanced management training program. He has also attended labor relations seminars at Stonehill College in North Easton, Massachusetts. He is studying at Akron University School of Law.

Recruited directly from college, Mr. Harris was promoted after five years as industrial relations representative (Akron Plant I) and manager of industrial relations with Firestone. He was born August 31, 1941 in Burnwell, West Virginia. He and his wife, Barbara, have no children. He is a stereo buff and enjoys bowling and golf.

Career Information

Training
Quite often labor relations managers have a law background with a specialization in labor law. Such an education provides a good basis for contract negotiations where legal language is highly important. College is becoming increasingly requisite for new entrants into labor relations, although larger industries maintain training institutes. Generally, a college degree in a social science, management or business is the best preparation for a career in labor relations.

Outlook
The growing complexity of business and government activities is expected to create a steadily expanding demand for those with labor law and labor relations training.

Additional Source Material
The American Management Association
135 W. 50th Street
New York, NY 10020

Society for Advancement of Management
1412 Broadway
New York, NY 10036

W. Lincoln Hawkins

Research Chemist

Dr. W. Lincoln Hawkins heads the Plastics Chemistry Research and Development Department at Bell Laboratories, in Murray Hill, New Jersey. He supervises applied research in plastics for telephone wire and cable, particularly the degradation and stabilization of plastics against heat, ultraviolet radiation, etc.

Born March 21, 1911 in Washington, D.C., Dr. Hawkins is a graduate of Rensselaer Polytechnic Institute (B.S., chemical engineering, 1932), Howard University (M.S., chemistry, 1932) and McGill University in Canada (Ph.D., chemistry, 1938).

Commenting on the opportunities for blacks in chemistry, he says: "It has been well established that black chemists can contribute significantly to chemical research." Opportunities for qualified blacks in the field will continue to increase, he believes.

Dr. Hawkins and his wife, Lilyan, have two sons, W. Gordon and Philip L. He enjoys gardening and sports.

Career Information

Training

Any type of research requires a strong chemistry background. For positions requiring a great deal of research responsibility, a Ph.D. is almost always a requisite. An advanced degree also increases the applicant's eligibility for faculty positions in colleges and universities. Most chemists having only the bachelor's degree begin their careers in industry or government where there are sometimes special training programs for new graduates. These programs supplement college training with specific industrial techniques and help determine the type of work for which the new employee is best suited.

Outlook

The employment outlook for chemists is expected to be favorable through the 1970s. In addition to new opportunities resulting from rapid growth, especially in research and development, thousands of new chemists will be needed every year to replace those lost through occupational turnover.

Additional Source Material

American Chemical Society
1155 16th Street, NW
Washington, DC 20036

Manufacturing Chemists' Association
1825 Connecticut Avenue, NW
Washington, DC 20009

Kenneth L. Hawthorne

Sales Manager

Kenneth L. Hawthorne is the New York City retail sales manager for Gulf Oil Company-U.S., headquartered in Lake Success, New York. He directs all retail sales through Gulf service stations in New York, New York, including gasoline, oil, tires, batteries and accesories. He supervises all sales personnel and makes decisions on promotions and real estate acquisitions. Previously, he held positions as retail consignment representative and Pennsylvania Turnpike sales supervisor. He was promoted to sales manager after eight years of employment. He has taken business courses and attended the Gulf Sales Training School. He gained experience as a service station operator for seventeen years. Though few blacks are in oil sales management, he says, oil companies are actively recruiting them for a variety of top positions.

Mr. Hawthorne was born February 16, 1934 in Mobile, Alabama. He is a member of Trendmakers of Pittsburgh and has worked with

90

disadvantaged minorities in job placement while on loan to the State of Pennsylvania's T.E.A.M. (Training Employment Assistance for Manpower) program. Mr. Hawthorne and his wife, Eugenia, have three children: Cecilia, Bruce and Bart. They live in Westbury, New York.

Career Information

Training

The salesman who sells complex goods or services may sometimes receive training that lasts for months. For some positions, salesmen must be college graduates who have majored in engineering or some other field. Still others gain experience through years of on-the-job training. Those who become managers in sales have a firm knowledge of that company's operating procedures plus the requisite managerial skills. Employers increasingly require beginning managers to have completed college. Although a person who does not have a degree may work his way up through the ranks, his promotional opportunities are becoming limited. For beginning management jobs, many employers look for persons who have a college degree in business administration with a major in accounting, economics or finance. Others look for applicants who have technical training in engineering, science or mathematics to deal with complex industrial processes. Still others hire liberal arts graduates and give them on-the-job training. Generally speaking, management training is an on-going thing, and experienced managers take advantage of college or management association offerings.

Outlook

New career opportunities for managers are expected to increase moderately through the 1970s. Many thousands of openings are also expected as a result of normal occupational fluctuations.

Additional Source Material

The American Management Association
135 W. 50th Street
New York, NY 10020

Society for the Advancement of Management
1412 Broadway
New York, NY 10036

Sales and Marketing Executives International
Student Education Division
630 Third Avenue
New York, NY 10017

David R. Hearon Jr.
Direct Purchase Engineering Manager

David R. Hearon Jr. is direct purchase engineering manager at Western Electric Company in Greensboro, North Carolina. He is responsible for the procurement and manufacture of computer peripheral equipment and trainer unique hardware for the Safeguard anti-ballistic missile system. He supervises forty-five persons. Previously, he was an engineer, an engineering department chief, and assistant manager for college relations.

92

Mr. Hearon has a B.S. degree in mechanical engineering from City College of New York, and has thirty credits toward an M.S. degree in business administration from the same school. He also has participated in a company graduate engineering training program and in advanced development management courses.

Blacks in engineering management are very rare, he says, but future opportunities are excellent. He and his wife, Barbara, have five children: David, Dana, Jonathan, Jeffrey and Sean.

Career Information

Training

As with other purchasing positions, many employers prefer to hire graduates of schools of business administration or engineering who have had courses in accounting, economics and purchasing. In a field as highly specialized as computer equipment purchasing, an extremely strong background in mechanical engineering is required. Many colleges and universities offer such degree programs. In terms of advancement, a college education is increasingly requisite, although it is possible to make entries without college on the basis of on-the-job experience.

Outlook

While the general opportunities for entry are rated as good, demand is expected to be excellent for graduates having backgrounds in engineering and science to fill jobs with firms that manufacture complex machinery, chemicals and other technical products.

Additional Source Material

The American Management Association
135 W. 50th Street
New York, NY 10020

Society for Advancement of Management
1412 Broadway
New York, NY 10036

Raymond K. Hill
Manager, Special Communications

Raymond Kent Hill is manager-special communications at General
Mills, Inc. in Minneapolis, Minnesota. He plans, organizes and
coordinates broad communications systems within the parent company
and its subsidiaries. He has a B.S. degree from Marymount College in

94

Kansas, and studied engineering at Kansas State University and at Wichita State University. He is studying for an M.B.A. degree and is taking specialized speech courses. He was born December 2, 1940 in Salina, Kansas. "Blacks are not rare in communications management," he says, "but opportunities are good to excellent, depending on the particular geographic area and company."

Mr. Hill and his wife, Eleanor, have two children, Kenton and Sonya.

Career Information

Training

Special communications jobs are often available at large corporations with many branches and subsidiaries. Special networks are required to link branches and subsidiaries with the home office. For most positions, a bachelor's degree in business administration, management, or a communications field (journalism) is a requirement for entry at the management level. Some companies may prefer to promote from within the ranks of its workers, but those promoted generally have a college background and are from personnel and related areas. Company-sponsored training programs or those offered at local colleges, universities and private organizations are available to maintain expertise.

Outlook

The employment outlook for personnel and company communication positions is expected to be good throughout the remainder of the decade. Although employment possibilities will probably be best for college graduates who have specialized training in personnel administration, positions will also be available for people with degrees in other areas.

Additional Source Material
American Society for Personnel Administration
19 Church Street
Berea, OH 44017

Hartsel F. Hilliard

Commercial Pilot

Hartsel F. "Steve" Hilliard is a pilot (second officer) with Eastern Airlines. He is based in New York, New York and assists the captain by performing such duties as monitoring electrical instruments and computing weight and balance forms, and by checking the interior and exterior of the plane before and after every flight.

Mr. Hilliard says that to qualify for a position as a pilot, one should have a college degree (preferably in a scientific area) and 1,500 flight hours with at least 100 in either jet or turbo jet aircraft. Military service training, he adds, is desirable for prospective commercial pilots. Commercial airlines usually recruit from the United States Air Force and the United States Navy. When he was hired by Eastern, Mr. Hilliard had 2,700 flight hours—one-third from military flying, another third

from civilian flying for the military, and the other third from flying for Southern Airways of Atlanta, Georgia.

Presently, there are fewer than 100 blacks among the more than 40,000 commercial pilots in the United States. However, Mr. Hilliard feels that opportunities are unlimited for blacks. "But it's difficult," he says. "The college degree and necessary flight experience take from seven to nine years of work, and many blacks don't dig the service."

Born February 2, 1943 in Weed, California, Mr. Hilliard is single and lives in Jamaica, Long Island, New York. He received a B.A. degree from the University of Washington in 1966. He joined the United States Army in 1966 and was discharged in 1969 as a captain. While in the army, he was awarded the Distinguished Flying Cross, the Bronze Star and thirteen air medals. He is a member of the Negro Airmen's International Association and the Air Line Pilots Association.

Career Information

Training
Pilots and co-pilots are licensed by the Federal Aviation Administration, commercial pilot licensees having at least two hundred hours of flight experience. For an instrument rating (for those who are subject to FAA instrument flight regulations or who anticipate flying on instruments in bad weather), applicants must have at least forty hours of instrument training, twenty of them in actual flight. Applicants for an airline transport license (carried by the captain on commercial trunk lines) must be at least twenty-three years old and must have at least 1,500 hours of flight time during the previous eight years, including night flying and instrument flying time. The requisite training may be obtained through military service or a private flying school. Advancement from co-pilot to captain often takes many years.

Outlook
A rapid rise in the employment of airline pilots is expected through the 1970s. Projected increases in passenger and cargo miles may exceed substantially the added capacity realized from new equipment. Therefore, employment will rise in response to this increase. Employment of pilots in general aviation activities is expected to grow very rapidly, particularly in business flying, aerial application, air-taxi operations and patrol and survey flying.

Additional Source Material
Air Line Pilots Association
1329 E Street, NW
Washington, DC 20004

Orenzo P. Hollowell Jr.

Computer Software Systems Analyst

Orenzo P. Hollowell Jr. is a computer software systems analyst at
Hart, Schaffner & Marx in Chicago, Illinois. He evaluates,
modifies, develops and implements computer software
(operating systems, computer language, packaged programs,
etc.) systems. Previously, he was a programmer and systems
analyst for the firm, one of the world's largest clothing manufacturers.
    Mr. Hollowell attended LeMoyne College in Memphis, Tennessee,

for one year and graduated from the Data Processing Institute. He considers opportunities in his field to be very good for blacks.

Married and the father of three children, Mr. Hollowell was born January 26, 1941 in Memphis. He enjoys bowling, music and woodcraft.

Career Information

Training
There is no universally acceptable way of preparing for work in systems analysis. Some employers prefer that candidates have a bachelor's degree and experience in mathematics, science, engineering, accounting or business. Other employers stress a graduate degree. Most employers, however, prefer to hire people with some experience in programming, which can be learned on the job, through courses at the firm or at outside schools. Educational preparation and experience often determine the kind of job opportunities available. Applicants may qualify on the basis of professional experience in scientific, technical or managerial occupations or practical experience in data processing jobs such as computer operator or programmer.

Outlook
Trends indicate excellent opportunities through the 1970s. Systems analysis has ranked among the fastest growing professional occupations in recent years. A growing demand for systems analysts will result from the rapid expansion of electronic data processing systems in business and government.

Additional Source Material
American Federation of Information
Processing Societies
210 Summit Avenue
Montvale, NJ 07645

Data Processing Management Association
505 Busse Highway
Park Ridge, IL 60068

Esther A. H. Hopkins

Research Chemist

Dr. Esther A. H. Hopkins supervises the emulsion coating and emulsion analysis laboratory at the Polaroid Corporation in Cambridge, Massachusetts. The laboratory checks the chemical composition of film coatings for uniformity. It also makes experimental films to order and analyzes them for certain components.

Born in Stamford, Connecticut, Dr. Hopkins is a graduate of Boston University (A.B., 1947), Howard University (M.S., chemistry, 1949) and Yale University (M.S., chemistry, 1962; Ph.D., chemistry 1967). Before she joined Polaroid in 1967, she was a research chemist at Stamford Research Labs of American Cyanamid (1959-61), an assistant in biophysics at the New England Institute for Medical Research in Ridgefield, Connecticut (1955-59), a control chemist at MRT, Inc. in Stamford (1954-55) and an instructor in chemistry at Virginia State College (1949-52).

Dr. Hopkins estimates that there are no more than 250 black chemists with Ph.D. degrees in the United States., and that only about

50 of them work in industry. About 8 percent of all chemists are women, she says. She believes that opportunities in the field are generally good for blacks.

Dr. Hopkins is a member of the board of directors of the Northeastern Section of the American Chemical Society. She is a member of the ACS National Council, a member of the council's standing committee on constitution and bylaws, and secretary of the ACS Women Chemists Committee. She is also a member of the Biophysics Society. An organist, she is a former dean of the Stamford Chapter of the American Guild of Organists. She and her husband, the Reverend T. Ewell Hopkins, live in Framingham, Massachusetts and have two children, Susan and Thomas.

Career Information

Training
This position requires a strong chemistry background. For positions requiring a great deal of research responsibility, a Ph. D. is almost always a requisite. According to the *Occupational Outlook Handbook,* published by the U.S. Bureau of Labor Statistics, the Ph. D. is generally required for research and for higher level faculty positions in a college or university, or for advancement to top-level positions in administration and other activities.

Outlook
Chemists will continue to be needed for research and development work. A slowdown in federal research and development, however, reflects anticipated reductions in the relative importance of the space and defense components of research and development. New graduates (with a bachelor's degree) will find openings in high school teaching—provided they have completed the necessary education courses and can meet other requirements for state certification. The greatest demand in colleges and universities will be for persons with Ph.D. degrees, with a smaller demand, particularly in junior colleges, for those with master's degrees.

Additional Source Material
American Chemical Society
1155 16th Street, NW
Washington, DC 20036

Manufacturing Chemists' Association, Inc.
1825 Connecticut Avenue, NW
Washington, DC 20009

James H. Jackson
Staff Operations Executive

James H. Jackson is staff operations executive at International
Telephone and Telegraph Company in New York, New York. He makes
monthly assessments of the ability of various IT&T companies to reach
their budgeted revenue and monthly, quarterly and year-end profit

goals. He also designs and implements plans that will enable the companies to improve their profit pictures.

Mr. Jackson has a B.A. degree in science education from the University of Northern Iowa, and he studied at Carleton College (in Minnesota) on a United Science Foundation Grant. He is a former member of the Iowa Legislature.

The future in profit and loss analysis, Mr. Jackson predicts, will be very bright for blacks. He is a member of the National Association of Manufacturers and Distribution and the Council of Concerned Black Executives. He was born April 24, 1939 in Waterloo, Iowa. He and his wife, Janet, have four daughters: Denise, Jacqueline, Stephanie and Christine. His leisure interests include hunting, fishing and bicycling.

Career Information

Training
This position falls under the larger field of corporate planning. Such jobs requiring facility in financial analysis are best qualified for with a college degree in business administration with a major in finance. Courses in economics, statistics and management are additional preparation.

Outlook
Positions leading to a management level in financial and profit planning will continue to be open throughout the 1970s. Industries are becoming increasingly concerned about long-range projections and are using the knowledge of trained financial specialists to provide them with an accurate picture of the future. Entry level positions such as financial researcher will be easiest to obtain for the college graduate.

Additional Source Material
The American Management Association
135 W. 50th Street
New York, NY 10020

Society for Advancement of Management
1412 Broadway
New York, NY 10036

Noel E. Jefferson
Sales Representative

Noel E. Jefferson is a sales representative at Eastern Airlines, Inc., in New York, New York. She serves as a liaison between Eastern's marketing and sales division and approximately 100 travel agencies throughout New York City. She keeps travel agents informed about new sales campaigns and services so that they may offer them to potential passengers.

The educational requirements for a sales representative position are becoming more demanding, Miss Jefferson says. Her own background includes studies at Ohio University and at the Eastern Airlines Training School. She also had on-the-job training, and she is completing work for a B.A. degree in social sciences at Herbert H. Lehman College of New York University.

Miss Jefferson, who is a member of Air Travel Executives Association, credits her own success in the field to "sales ability" and says that any black with excellent salesmanship techniques, marketing knowledge, college training and a sales background would qualify for a management position in sales. She was born November 27, 1945 in Cincinnati, Ohio, and now lives in the Bronx, New York. She enjoys photography, water skiing, theater, travel, and writing short stories.

Career Information

Training
The best preparation for a managerial position in sales is a college degree in marketing, business administration, finance or a related field. The entire field of sales and marketing contains so many subfields that, often, specialization comes after entry-level experience on the job. Persons seeking entrance into management training programs are best suited with a college degree in one of the above mentioned areas. See the *Training* section under other marketing and sales occupations.

Outlook
The outlook for the rest of the decade in sales—all fields—is excellent. With the development of special markets—youth, ethnic groups and minorities, and the aged—employers will be looking for trainees with solid backgrounds for channeling toward a specialty.

Additional Source Material
American Marketing Association
230 North Michigan Avenue
Chicago, IL 60601

The American Management Association
135 W. 50th Street
New York, NY 10020

S. Preston Jones

Patent Agent

S. Preston Jones, a patent agent with Dow Chemical Company in Midland, Michigan, provides complete patent services to the research and business area of the company. Specifically, he obtains patents for inventions resulting from research. He also assists in training new employees. Dow is a major manufacturer of chemicals for use in agriculture pharmacy, environmental health, etc. Its annual gross is $2 billion.

A 1956 graduate of Hampton Institute with a B.S. degree in chemistry, Mr. Jones was a patent examiner in the United States Patent Office for twelve years before joining Dow. He was recruited by the company's Patent Department. "There are 10,500 registered patent solicitors, but less than 1 percent of those are black," he says. "Many blacks don't trust private industry to treat them fairly in this field; they prefer to remain with, or seek employment with, governmental agencies which are protected by civil service." However, he says opportunities are very good for blacks who have a scientific background. "They are even better for those with a law degree," he says. Mr. Jones was born June 2, 1935 in Jacksonville, Florida. He and his wife, Betty, have two sons, Allen and Anthony. He enjoys photography, folk music and bowling.

Career Information

Training
Patent law is among the areas of specialization in the law field. In spite of the fact that some opportunities exist for those without law degrees, that number is dwindling as more graduates of law schools apply for positions. The training is that for most law students, with the first two years generally devoted to fundamental courses such as contracts, criminal law, property law and judicial procedure. In the third year, students elect courses in specialized fields such as tax, labor or corporation law.

Outlook
Salaried employment, such as patent counsel, will be limited mainly to the metropolitan areas where the chief employers of legal talent—government agencies, corporations and law firms—are concentrated. For many able and well-qualified lawyers, opportunities to advance will be available in both salaried employment and private practice.

Additional Source Material
Information Service
The American Bar Association
1155 E. 60th Street
Chicago, IL 60637

Association of American Law Schools
Suite 370
1 Dupont Circle, NW
Washington, DC 20036

Joyce A. Ladner

Associate Professor of Sociology

Joyce A. Ladner is an associate professor of sociology at Howard University, Washington, D.C. She teaches courses to both graduate and undergraduate students, specializing in intergroup relations, social deviance, socialization of the child and socialization of the black woman.

A graduate of Tougaloo College in Mississippi, Miss Ladner earned both her master's and doctorate degrees at Washington University, St. Louis, Missouri. A former research associate at the University of Dar es Salaam, Tanzania, Miss Ladner has written a book, *Tomorrow's Tomorrow—The Black Woman.*

Born October 12, 1943, in Waynesboro, Mississippi, Miss Ladner calls her approach to life "pragmatic," citing her Mississippi childhood as responsible. "That Southern background always taught me (and forced me) to constantly relate to observable phenomena and to look for practical results."

Miss Ladner lives in Washington and spends her leisure time attending plays and movies.

Career Information

Training
To qualify for most beginning positions in colleges and universities, applicants must have at least a master's degree, and for many, must have completed all requirements for the doctorate except the dissertation. Also for teaching, specialization in some field is necessary, plus undergraduate courses in humanities, social sciences, natural sciences and the mastery of at least one foreign language. Intensive training in the specialization area is given in graduate school, where some students receive practical experience as teaching assistants. Financial aid assistance is particularly abundant for those attending schools of education in state systems.

Outlook
College teaching opportunities are expected to be good for those having completed the Ph.D. or all the requirements thereof except the dissertation. Opportunities will be best in junior colleges for those having only a master's degree.

Additional Source Material
American Association of University Professors
One Dupont Circle, NW
Washington, DC 20036

American Council on Education
One Dupoint Circle, NW
Washington, DC 20036

American Federation of Teachers
1012 14th Street, NW
Washington, DC 20005

National Education Association
1201 16th Street, NW
Washington, DC 20036

Norval Constantine Lamb
Design Engineer

Norval Constantine Lamb, a design engineer for the Joseph Schlitz Brewing Co. in Milwaukee, Wisconsin, supervises the design and installation of equipment used to supply utilities for brewery needs. He also conducts waste evaluation testing programs at all of the company's branch plants.

Previously a project engineer, Mr. Lamb gained experience while working as a design engineer for Procon Inc. in Chicago, Ill.; Morgen Design, Inc. in Milwaukee; and Kaiser Aluminum Co. in Kingston, Jamaica. He is a graduate of Milwaukee Area Technical College (associate degree, chemistry) and the University of Chicago (B.S., mechanical engineering). He considers as his most significant achievement his tutoring of three high school students who received academic scholarships to major universities.

Born in January, 1939 in Kingston, Jamaica, Mr. Lamb enjoys reading, photography and music in his spare time. He and his wife, Nettie, have three children.

110

Career Information

Training

Design engineering is an application rather than a separate branch of the much larger field of engineering. For background, a particular design engineering job may require electrical engineering training, especially when the job calls for facilities for generating and distributing electrical power. In general, however, a B.S. degree in engineering is the accepted educational requirement for entrance into engineering positions. Well-qualified graduates having training in physics, or in one of the other natural sciences or mathematics, may qualify for some beginning positions in engineering. Only a small number of persons without a degree are able to become engineers after long experience in a related field—such as drafting or engineering technology—and some college level training. Advanced training is being emphasized for an increasing number of jobs. Graduate degrees are required for teaching and research positions and for advancement. About 270 colleges, universities and engineering schools offer 1000 engineering curricula choices.

Outlook

The outlook for new engineers during the 1970s is favorable. Engineers who are not well-grounded in the fundamentals, and whose specialization is narrow, could be adversely affected by shifts in defense activities and rapidly changing technology. Demand probably will be strong for new graduates who have acquired recently developed techniques—including computer applications—and for engineers who can apply engineering principles to medical, biological and other sciences.

Additional Source Material

Engineers' Council for Professional Development
345 E. 47th Street
New York, NY 10017

Engineering Manpower Commission
Engineers Joint Council
345 E. 47th Street
New York, NY 10017

National Society of Professional Engineers
2029 K Street, NW
Washington, DC 20006

Nancy Lane

Executive Recruiter

Nancy Lane is a second vice president at Chase Manhattan
Bank, North America, in New York, New York. She is interested in
linking students at black colleges with black executives in major
corporations, and has created such a program in her position
as head of executive staff recruitment for the bank, one of the
world's largest. A native of Boston, Massachusetts, she has
a B.S. degree from Boston University and an M.S. degree in public
administration from the University of Pittsburgh. Miss Lane believes
that opportunities will increase at an accelerated pace for blacks
in banking. A member of the Council of Concerned Black
Executives, she is interested in "volunteer activities tied with
educational programs aimed at black students." Miss Lane is
single. Her leisure interests include travel and theater.

112

Career Information

Training
In general, executive recruiting is a position created in response to the trend toward high specialization. As a profession, it belongs under the broader "personnel" category. The training requirements for executive recruiting depend largely upon the company where the position is held. In banking, at least a rudimentary knowledge of finance is helpful, but a general assessment of qualifications suggests an undergraduate degree in personnel or public administration.

Outlook
College graduates who enter personnel work are expected to find many opportunities through the 1970s. Although employment prospects probably will be best for college graduates who have specialized training in personnel administration, positions will be available for people having degrees in other fields.

Additional Source Material
American Society for Personnel Administration
19 Church Street
Berea, OH 44017

Vernice McGriff
Planning Manager

Vernice McGriff is manager of corporate business planning at Radio Corporation of America in New York, New York. Her responsibilities include assessment and review of the annual business plan for each division of RCA (National Broadcasting Company, Hertz Rent-A-Car, Banquet Foods, and Consumer Electronics are a few), giving special attention to marketing plans and strategy.

Mrs. McGriff, who was born in Newark, New Jersey, has a B.S. degree in marketing from New York University, and has taken graduate courses at NYU's Bernard Baruch Graduate School. She has also had on-the-job training, and worked as a product manager and marketing researcher with other firms. She believes that her job is rare for black women, but that larger corporations will gradually offer additional positions in corporate planning.

Mrs. McGriff, a widow, has a daughter, Lori.

Career Information

Training

Long-range corporate planning is something that large companies, especially, are engaging in to an ever-increasing degree. A bachelor's degree is the usual requirement to become a marketing research trainee. A master's degree in business administration is becoming more desirable, especially for advancement to higher level positions. As they gain experience, those in entry-level positions may advance to higher positions with responsibility for specific marketing research projects and, eventually, to top managerial positions. Be sure to check training requirements listed under other managerial occupations.

Outlook

College graduates trained in marketing research and statistics are likely to find favorable job opportunities in this field throughout the 1970s. The increase in marketing services and the need for companies to make long-range plans to meet the needs of growing markets are creating the demand.

Additional Source Material
American Marketing Association
230 North Michigan Avenue
Chicago, IL 60601

Nampeo D. R. McKenney

Demographic Specialist

Nampeo D. R. McKenney is a demographic specialist for the Bureau of the Census in Washington, D.C. She heads a staff which collects and publishes reports on the racial population of the United States pertaining to ethnic origin and nationality. Mrs. McKenney's department is also responsible for the publication of an annual census report on the social and economic characteristics of blacks. These data often provide the basis for federal social action programs instituted in the black community.

The holder of a master's degree in demographic sociology from American University, Washington, D.C., Mrs. McKenney was nominated in 1972 for the Federal Woman's award, one of the highest commendations given to women in government. According to Mrs. McKenney, demographics is "a wide open field" for blacks, and many are needed in this specialized area.

Born September 25, 1938, in Washington, D.C., Mrs. McKenney lives with her husband Martin and daughter Gilesa in Baltimore, Maryland. She enjoys gardening in her spare time.

Career Information

Training

Demographics is a social science dealing with characteristics of populations and requires a strong sociology and economics background. A master's degree is a minimum requirement for employment as a demographic sociologist. The doctorate is essential for teaching positions in most colleges or universities and is commonly required for the heads of major research projects, important administrative positions or consultants. The choice of a graduate school is very important for people planning to become sociologists. Students interested in research should select schools which emphasize training in research methods and statistics, and provide opportunities to gain practical experience in research work.

Outlook

Employment opportunities for sociologists with doctorates are expected to be good during the 1970s. Those having only a master's degree are likely to face considerable competition. Sociologists well-trained in research methods and advanced statistics will have the widest choice of jobs. Most positions foreseen will be in college teaching, hence the Ph.D. requirement.

Additional Source Material

The American Sociological Association
1001 Connecticut Avenue, NW
Washington, D. C. 20036

John J. Mance
Industrial Relations Administrator

John J. Mance is assistant to the director of industrial relations at Lockheed-California Company in Burbank, California. He administers and monitors the company's Affirmative Action Program, and develops other programs designed to enhance employment and promotion opportunities for minorities and females at the huge aircraft manufacturing firm. He also serves as a liaison between the company and various government agencies, and is chairman of the Affirmative Action Council.

Mr. Mance has an aeronautical engineering diploma from Cal-Aero Technical Institute in Glendale, California, an industrial relations certificate from the University of California at Los Angeles, a Lockheed management certificate from Lockheed Management Institute at the

University of Southern California, and a certificate from the Managerial Policy Institute at USC. Although his training was not specifically for his present job, he says that previous experience in industrial relations and a good knowledge of civil rights were beneficial. He had been a Lockheed industrial relations manager, personnel programs representative, and employment interviewer.

He coordinated the hiring, training and orientation of more than two hundred employees, mainly blacks, from south Los Angeles and Compton for work at the Lockheed Watts-Willowbrook plant. Mr. Mance was born March 18, 1926 in Chicago, Illinois. He and his wife, Eleanore, have two sons, Richard and David. They live in Granada Hills, California. Mr. Mance is active in the NAACP.

Career Information

Training

Industrial relations can encompass a wide range of responsibilities depending on the size of the company. In any case, a college degree in management, business administration or personnel management, or a liberal arts degree with courses in management, facilitates entry. On-the-job training is available at most companies, or employees attend industrial relations courses at local colleges or universities. Those with grounding in labor law have an advantage. In cases where the position originates from federal legislation, as in Affirmative Action Programs, employees become familiar with appropriate laws through company training institutes.

Outlook

Many employers are recognizing the importance of good employee relations. Thus they are depending more heavily on the services of trained personnel workers.

Additional Source Material

American Society for Personnel Administration
19 Church Street
Berea, OH 44017

Government careers in personnel

Public Personnel Association
1313 E. 60th Street
Chicago, IL 60637

Robert C. Maynard

Newspaper Executive

Robert C. Maynard is associate editor and ombudsman of *The Washington Post* newspaper in Washington, D.C. He is the sole individual responsible for monitoring the performance of the newspaper and the news media generally for fairness, responsiveness and accuracy. His is the most prestigious position held by any black man on a daily newspaper in the United States. Prior to his appointment in 1972 he was a national correspondent and, earlier, a metropolitan reporter.

Born June 17, 1937 in Brooklyn, N.Y., Mr. Maynard rejected the traditional approaches to a career in journalism; at fifteen he simply dropped out of high school and "devoted myself singly to becoming the best writer I could become." He steeped himself in the classics, in American literature and black history—"and I wrote, wrote, wrote."

After scouring the country for a job, he was hired in 1951 by the *Gazette and Daily* newspaper in York, Pennsylvania. His excellent work led to a Nieman Fellowship in journalism at Harvard University (1965–66). The fellowship is his only academic credential. In 1972 he was co-director (with Earl Caldwell of *The New York Times*) of the Summer Program for Minority Group Members at Columbia University Graduate School of Journalism.

Divorced, Mr. Maynard has a daughter, Dori. In his spare time, he enjoys hiking, woodcarving and photography.

Career Information

Training
The position of newspaper editor is usually achieved by journalists after years of experience. For beginning writing positions, many newspapers will consider only applicants having a college education. Some editors prefer graduates who have a degree in journalism. Other employers find a liberal arts degree equally acceptable. Professional studies leading to a degree in journalism are offered at nearly 200 colleges, and over 250 junior colleges offer journalism programs.

Outlook
Well-qualified beginners with exceptional writing talent will find favorable employment opportunities through the 1970s. Editors will also be looking for reporters who are qualified to handle news about highly specialized or technical subjects.

Additional Source Material
American Newspaper Publishers Association
750 Third Avenue
New York, NY 10017

The Newspaper Fund, Inc.
Box 300
Princeton, NJ 08540

American Council on Education for Journalism
School of Journalism
University of Missouri
Columbia, MO 65201

Octavia Leah Miles

Product Planner

Octavia L. Miles is an associate product planner and competitive analyst at Mattel Toy Co., Hawthorne, Calif. She makes analyses of which competitive products are important each year in terms of sales and advertising costs. She also studies and reports on other toy industries—their sales strengths and weaknesses and their advertising strategies.

Mrs. Miles' first job as advertising and sales promotion coordinator gave her experience in budgeting, design, print buying and lithography. A graduate of Michigan State University with a bachelor of science degree in history, she also holds a master of arts from the University of Chicago in history. While at the University of Southern California, she completed three marketing courses and participated in a media planning workshop in 1970. A year later, in New York City, she participated in a television cost control seminar. Although opportunities in marketing for blacks exist, she said, "the prospects are not too rosy at the moment."

Mrs. Miles, who was born in Boston, Massachusetts on April 28, 1938, is a widow and lives in Los Angeles, California with her twelve-year-old son. In her leisure time she enjoys swimming, hiking, tennis.

122

Career Information

Training
Marketing is a large field that has experienced the major part of its growth in the last fifteen years. There are many facets to it, most of which require a general background and specialized on-the-job training. A product planner must have a knowledge of budgeting and financial analysis methods. There are design requirements most of which can be filled by attending a company-sponsored institute or departments of advertising design at local colleges and universities. Many schools in the United States offer advertising sales courses and courses in the visual media such as graphic design. The best background for people interested in product planning on the entry level is a bachelor's degree in business administration or marketing, with a minor or additional study in design.

Outlook
Occupational prospects are expected to be good throughout the remainder of the decade. Companies are finding it increasingly necessary to engage the help of market planners to keep pace with spiraling consumerism. Employment will be easier to find for those with an undergraduate degree in the appropriate field.

Additional Source Material
American Marketing Association
230 N. Michigan Avenue
Chicago, IL 60601

Sales and Marketing Executives International
Student Education Division
630 Third Avenue
New York, NY 10017

Dr. Evelyn M. Mobley

Chief of Health Services

Evelyn M. Mobley, M.D., is chief of the Health Services Branch at the
U.S. Air Force Medical Center, Wright-Patterson Air Force Base, Ohio.
In the Civilian Employee Health Services Division, she is responsible for
the health, education and welfare of some 28,000 military and civilian
employees through industrial and preventive medicine.

A graduate of Ohio State University with a bachelor of science in
bacteriology, Dr. Mobley received her doctor of medicine degree in 1960
from Meharry Medical School, Nashville, Tennessee. Dr. Mobley, who
was a medical officer with the army prior to her present position,
estimates that her job is rare for a black person, but that future
opportunities for blacks are good in all health-related fields.

Dr. Mobley was born September 21, 1933, in Pittsburgh,
Pennsylvania. She and her husband, also a doctor, have two children.
Dr. Mobley is a bridge-player and ice-skater in her spare time.

124

Career Information

Training
Physicians require a great deal of training, usually eight years beyond secondary school. Because a license is required to practice medicine in all states and the District of Columbia, all candidates must pass a licensing exam and (in 33 of the states and Washington, D.C.) serve a one-year hospital internship. Most of the 90-plus approved medical schools require applicants to have completed at least three years of college. Premedical study must include undergraduate courses in English, physics, biology and inorganic and organic chemistry. Students should acquire a broad general education in the humanities, mathematics and the social sciences. The first two years upon entrance into medical school are generally spent in labs and classrooms learning basic medical sciences such as anatomy, biochemistry, physiology, pharmacology, microbiology and pathology. The last two years are spent in hospitals and clinics for practical experience.

Outlook
Excellent opportunities are expected for physicians through the seventies. Increased demand for physicians' services will result from such factors as population growth, rising numbers of older persons (the age group requiring extensive physicians' services), increased health consciousness of the public and the trend toward higher standards of health care.

Additional Source Material
Council on Medical Education
American Medical Association
535 No. Dearborn Street
Chicago, IL 60610

Association of American Medical Colleges
1 Dupont Circle, NW
Washington, DC 20036

Clarence R. Mosley

Engineer

Clarence R. Mosley is an engineer at General Telephone Company of California in Santa Monica, California. He assists in the development of procedures and standards relating to electronic tool switching equipment and provides technical support for equipment construction and service and service personnel in testing and "debugging" initial installation of the equipment. Previously, he was a wage and salary analyst and an equipment engineer. He has a B.S. degree in electrical engineering from California State College and has taken various electronics courses. Mr. Mosley estimates that opportunities in communications engineering will be good for blacks during the 1970s.

126

Born September 7, 1932, in Fort Worth, Texas, Mr. Mosley is married and has two children. When he is not spending time with his family, photography, sport cars and electronics occupy his free time. A committed engineer, he explains, "There is a terrible waste of human resources in this country and the world, and we could make this world a better place for this generation and future generations if we were able to make better use of our most important resource."

Career Information

Training
Electrical engineers usually specialize in a major area of work such as electronics, electrical equipment manufacturing, communications or power. (Check under *Training* in other engineering occupations for beginning educational requirements.)

Outlook
Employment prospects for electrical engineers engaged in communications equipment development are anticipated to be very good over the next few years. The growing need for more efficient communications is the cause for this increase in opportunities.

Additional Source Material
Institute of Electrical and Electronic Engineers
345 E. 47th Street
New York, NY 10017

Herbert W. Neal

Marketing Strategy Coordinator

Herbert W. Neal is a strategy coordinator for decaffeinated coffees at General Foods Corporation in White Plains, New York. He coordinates marketing strategies for the Sanka and Brim brands. Previously, he was product manager for Sanka. Born July 30, 1929 in Boston, Massachusetts, Mr. Neal has a bachelor's degree in economics from Harvard University (1949) and an M.B.A. degree from Harvard Business School (1953). During an eighteen-month period ending in 1972, he was on leave from General Foods, serving the United States Department of Health, Education and Welfare as deputy regional director for the New York region (New York, New Jersey, Puerto Rico and the United States Virgin Islands).

128

Mr. Neal believes that "opportunities in the food industry are favorable for blacks at this time." In his spare time, Mr. Neal enjoys landscaping and bridge. He is president of the Board of Education of Pequanneck Township, New Jersey. Elected to the position in 1969, he has been a member of the board since 1963. He and his wife, Sue, have two children, Alita and Todd.

Career Information

Training

A position such as "stragegy coordinator" demonstrates the complexity of the marketing process. Each product manufactured by some large companies has a staff dedicated to the most efficient and effective selling of that product. Training, as with other marketing positions, consists mainly of a marketing degree at the entry level. Once a person obtains a position within a given company, performance on the job, experience and additional specialized training (offered through the company or at local colleges and universities) are the keys to advancement (see *Training* under other marketing and sales occupations).

Outlook

The outlook for positions in marketing (especially specialized jobs) will remain high during the 1970s. College graduates with backgrounds in statistics, economics and related fields will find the opportunities especially good.

Additional Source Material

American Marketing Association
230 North Michigan Avenue
Chicago, IL 60601

Sales and Marketing Executives International
Student Education Division
630 Third Avenue
New York, NY 10017

Edward O. Nelson
Environmental Technician

Edward O. Nelson operates and maintains one of six continuous air monitoring stations for the U. S. Environmental Protection Agency. Mr. Nelson operates a one-man station near St. Louis, Missouri, sampling pollution levels, and field-testing new equipment aimed at improving pollution monitoring techniques. He also trains other technicians.

Mr. Nelson received the bulk of his training through courses offered by the EPA. When he started with the agency, "The instrumentation was prototype," Mr. Nelson says, "and I was given the operation manuals and told to learn them." Since that time, he has attended factory and technical schools to keep abreast of developing technology. Mr. Nelson is also attending the evening division of Washington University (St. Louis) for a degree in computer electronics.

With a long-standing interest in electronics, Mr. Nelson worked as a radio engineer at a local radio station in addition to his full-time job. He has a first class radio license and is an amateur radio operator. Mr. Nelson recommends his field to young black people. The future holds unlimited opportunities for those who are qualified, and universities and colleges are now offering degrees in environmental studies.

130

Born February 2, 1925 in Johnsonville, Tennessee, Mr. Nelson now lives with his wife, Pauline, in St. Louis. The couple have six children.

Career Information

Training
Young people who wish to prepare for careers as engineering or science technicians can obtain the necessary training from a great variety of education institutions or can qualify for their work right on the job. Most employes, however, seek workers who have had some form of specialized training for more responsible technician jobs. Specialized formal training programs are offered in post-secondary schools—technical institutes, junior and community colleges, area vocational-technical schools and extension divisions of colleges and universities—as well as in technical and technical-vocational high schools. Other ways in which people can become qualified include on-the-job training, work experience and part-time schooling, correspondence schools or through training in the armed forces.

Outlook
Employment for engineering and science technicians is expected to be very good for the rest of the decade. The demand will be strongest for graduates of post-secondary school technician training programs. Well-qualified women technicians should continue to find favorable employment opportunities, chiefly in designing jobs, chemical and other laboratory work and in computation and other work requiring the application of mathematics.

Additional Source Material
American Society for Engineering Education
Suit 400
1 Dupont Circle
Washington, DC 20036

National Council of Technical Schools
1835 K Street, NW
Room 907
Washington, DC 20006

Engineers' Council for Professional
 Development
345 E. 47th Street
New York, NY 10017

Nathaniel B. Nelson
Chief Reservations Supervisor

Nathaniel B. Nelson is chief supervisor-reservations at Eastern
Airlines, Inc. in Woodbridge, New Jersey. He directs ten supervisors
(each with a team of 20 reservations agents) in airline reservations
functions and is primarily concerned with solving personnel problems.
He obtained the position after six years as a reservations agent and a
supervisor of executive accounts. He is studying at Rutgers University
for a B.S. degree in marketing.

Black chief supervisors are rare, says Mr. Nelson, but future
opportunities in the field are unlimited.

132

Mr. Nelson was born August 15, 1936 in New Canaan, Connecticut. He now lives in Englewood, New Jersey, with his wife, Maude, and two children, Bruce and Melanie. In his spare time, he enjoys basketball, photography, travel and camping.

Career Information

Training
Reservations supervisors generally start in lower positions with the company. Because agents and clerks often deal directly with the public, airlines have strict hiring standards with respect to appearance, personality and education. High school graduation is required, and college training is considered desirable. College courses in transportation—such as traffic management and air transportation, as well as experience in other areas of air transportation—are helpful for a higher grade job such as traffic representative. Traffic agents may advance to representative or supervisor.

Outlook
Positions for traffic personnel will increase rapidly over the next several years, mainly because of increased passenger and cargo traffic. Mechanization will adversely affect reservations clerks, however. The employment of ticket agents whose main job involves personal contacts will not be affected very much although their paper work will be reduced considerably. The small group of traffic representatives probably will increase substantially as airlines compete for new business.

Additional Source Material
Air Line Employees Association
5600 So. Central Avenue
Chicago, IL 60638

Placid Jean Parker

Nursing Instructor

Placid Jean Parker is an instructor in medical-surgical nursing at the Buffalo General Hospital in Buffalo, New York. She supervises instruction and clinical laboratory experience, counsels and evaluates progress of the nursing students assigned to her for instruction. She also links her teaching to a knowledge of the community to enrich the learning experience of her students.

Mrs. Parker, the first black to teach at Buffalo General, attended Provident Hospital School of Nursing in Baltimore, Maryland, and was licensed as a registered nurse in the state in 1947. Since then, she has taken courses in supervision and management, completed her bachelor of science degree in nursing from D'Youville College, Buffalo, New York, and earned a certificate in disaster nursing. Before joining the staff of Buffalo General, Mrs. Parker served as an assistant head nurse at Millard Fillmore Hospital and as head nurse and supervisor at Children's Hospital, both in Buffalo. Her experience ranges from outpatient nursing to neurologic and orthopedic nursing.

An active community and church organizer, Mrs. Parker advocates a philosophy of hard work. "If you try hard enough, have a thirst for knowledge and possess a quality of great determination, you will succeed." Born March 5, 1925, she and her husband, Juan C., have three children: Juan C. Jr., Gene Pierre and Lynn Elizabeth.

Career Information

Training

A license is required to practice professional nursing in all states and the District of Columbia. To obtain a license, a nurse must have graduated from a school approved by the state board of nursing and must pass a board examination. Three types of programs offer the basic education required for registered nursing—diploma, baccalaureate and associate. The first is offered at hospitals and independent schools of nursing and generally requires three years of attendance. Baccalaureate degrees are obtained from colleges and universities and require four (or sometimes five) years of training. Associate degrees are offered at junior and community colleges after two years of study. There are more than 1,300 programs of these types available in the United States. In addition, about seventy schools award master's and doctoral degrees in nursing. Students interested should also check the sections on state and medical field aid elsewhere in this book; financial backing is available from many sources.

Outlook

Employment opportunities for registered nurses are expected to be very good for the near future. Increased public health services, the rise in the population, better hospitalization plans and advanced medical technology all contribute to the need for more nurses. Those with graduate degrees will find ample opportunities in administration, teaching, research, public health nursing and other specializations.

Additional Source Material

ANA-NLN Committee on Nursing Careers
American Nurses' Association
10 Columbus Circle
New York, NY 10019

For information on employment in the Veterans Administration:
Department of Medicine and Surgery
Veterans Administration
Washington, DC 20420

James C. Partridge Jr.
Library Specialist

James C. Partridge Jr. manages the operation of the Maryland State
Library for the Physically Handicapped. As specialists in library
services, Mr. Partridge and his staff have complete charge of 25,000
books, including talking books, magnetic and cassette tapes distributed
to the blind and handicapped throughout the state of Maryland. Nearly
five thousand readers are served.

Since he has been with the Maryland State Library, Mr. Partridge has tripled the number of persons receiving library material. He earned a bachelor of arts degree in sociology from Morehouse College, Atlanta, and a master of library science from Atlanta University. He has also done additional work in special education at Coppin State College, Baltimore.

Mr. Partridge estimates that of the fifty regional libraries for the blind and handicapped throughout the United States, blacks employed number fewer than five. Opportunities are limitless, however.

Born in Atlanta, Georgia, on May 13, 1940, Mr. Partridge is single and lives in Baltimore. In his spare moments, he likes to restore old houses and collect records.

Career Information

Training

To qualify as a professional librarian, an applicant must ordinarily complete a one-year master's degree program in library science. A Ph.D. is an advantage to those who plan a teaching career in library schools or who aspire to top administrative posts. Nearly fifty schools in the United States are accredited by the American Library Association, and many other colleges offer courses within their four-year undergraduate programs, as well as at the graduate level, which prepare students for some type of library work.

Outlook

The employment outlook for trained librarians is expected to be good through the seventies. The best chances will probably be in school, college and university libraries. Persons who have only a bachelor's degree with a major in library science will face stiff competition; most openings require a graduate degree.

Additional Source Material

American Library Association
50 E. Huron Street
Chicago, IL 60611

Special Libraries Association
235 Park Avenue, South
New York, NY 10003

American Society for Information Science
1140 Constitution Avenue, NW
Washington, DC 20202

James E. Payne
Package Administrator

James E. Payne is associate package administrator at Avon Products, Inc. in New York, New York. He oversees the development of packages from design approval to final production. His responsibility involves making decisions regarding the "look" and "feel" of the package to insure ultimate consumer acceptance.

Mr. Payne was born March 23, 1941 in Mississippi. He has a B.S. degree in education from Jackson (Miss.) State College. He was a senior employment administrator at Avon before being promoted to his present position in 1972.

138

Mr. Payne's position is unique in the cosmetics industry and is a rare one for blacks. He estimates only ''fair'' job opportunities in his field in the future. He says that there is no way to acquire formal training for his job ''since few, if any, colleges offer courses in what I'm doing.''

Besides spending time with his wife, Judith, and children, Karen and Stephanie, Mr. Payne enjoys photography and reading.

Career Information

Training

There is no standard recommendation for educational prerequisites, but as with all marketing positions, a bachelor's degree in marketing or related fields is acceptable. A master's degree in business administration is also becoming increasingly desirable. Many people can qualify through previous experience, but for the new entrant, a college degree or some college training is more rewarding. Some courses in graphic arts and design, available at junior and community colleges and technical schools, also make good foundations for positions where design and visual presentation are involved.

Outlook

New entrants and trainees will find favorable opportunities in marketing fields throughout the 1970s. Employment prospects are the brightest for the highly qualified college graduate.

Additional Source Material

American Marketing Association
230 North Michigan Avenue
Chicago, IL 60601

Eugene Pickens

Bank Executive

Eugene Pickens is an assistant treasurer and corporate lending officer at Chase Manhattan Bank in New York, New York. He is responsible for maintaining corporate customers, developing new customer relationships and marketing various services of the bank. He sometimes offers financial counselling to corporations requesting multi-million dollar loans.

Mr. Pickens was born September 19, 1944 in Sawyerville, Alabama. After graduating from Tennessee State University in 1970 with a B.S. degree in business administration, he was hired by Chase Manhattan through the college placement office at TSU. His on-the-job training consisted of an eighteen-month training program for corporate lending officers—a program in which he studied all phases of financial analysis, accounting and marketing. He later attended the New York University Graduate School of Business.

Blacks in commercial banking are rare; Mr. Pickens is the first black lending officer in the National Division at Chase Manhattan, the third largest bank in the United States. Opportunities in banking are excellent for blacks, he believes.

Mr. Pickens and his wife, Jewel, live in Union City, New Jersey. He enjoys skiing and basketball.

140

Career Information

Training
Loan officers must be familiar with economics, production, distribution, merchandising, and commercial law. Bank officer positions may be filled by management trainees or by promoting experienced clerical employees. Outstanding clerks may be selected in spite of limited educational background, but college graduation is usually a requirement for management trainees. A business administration major in finance or a liberal arts curriculum including accounting, economics, commercial law, political science and statistics serves as excellent preparation for officer trainee positions. Special study, particularly that offered by the American Institute of Banking, is often helpful to advancement.

Outlook
The number of bank officers is expected to increase rapidly through the 1970s as banking activities expand. Increased use of computers enables banks to analyze and plan banking operations more extensively and to provide new kinds of services. Although college graduates who meet the standards for executive trainees should find good opportunities for entry positions, many officer positions will be filled by promotions from within. Competition for these promotions, particularly in large banks, will be keen.

Additional Source Material
American Bankers Association
Personnel Administration and
Management Development
1120 Connecticut Avenue, NW
Washington, DC 20036

National Association of Bank Women, Inc.
National Office
111 E. Wacker Drive
Chicago, IL. 60601

National Bankers Association
4310 Georgia Avenue, NW
Washington, DC 20011

James O. Plinton Jr.
Travel Marketing Vice President

James O. Plinton Jr. is division vice president-special marketing affairs at Eastern Airlines, Inc., in Miami, Florida. He designs action programs for development of travel markets for Eastern, one of the world's largest airlines.

Mr. Plinton is a graduate of Lincoln University (B.S., science, 1935) and attended the University of Newark (N.J.) Division of Aeronautics. During World War II he was a flight instructor at Tuskegee Institute and was a member of the 99th Pursuit Squadron. After the war he was a commercial pilot. For fifteen years he was on the executive administrative and marketing staff of Trans World Airlines. He joined Eastern in 1971.

The airline industry, Mr. Plinton believes, probably offers blacks "the most promising future of any industry and is becoming more diversified."

Mr. Plinton was born July 22, 1914 in Westfield, New Jersey. He was knighted by the Haitian government and has received honors and awards from a number of universities and fraternities. He is a member of five boards of directors as well as numerous professional, fraternal and social organizations. He and his wife, Kathryn, have two children, James III and Kathy Ann. They live in Miami. In his leisure time he listens to music and participates in water sports.

Career Information

Training
Many industries that offer goods and services have discovered the need to appeal to special markets such as ethnic groups and the young. For this reason, they have developed departments of special marketing and seek qualified persons to head them. The educational requirements for such a position differ from company to company, but it is possible to pinpoint specific areas where potential employers seek expertise (see *Training* under other sales and marketing occupations). For entry into such a position, those interested should have a bachelor's degree in business administration, marketing, economics or other related fields. A good knowledge of statistical analysis methods is also useful. For a specialization such as special marketing affairs, some experience in other marketing areas is excellent background. In most cases, the company will offer training orientation institutes, and often will sponsor a promising employee at local colleges or universities where courses are offered.

Outlook
The demand for specialists is likely to continue throughout the 1970s, and those with a college background are in a good position to obtain what available positions there will be.

Additional Source Material
American Marketing Association
230 North Michigan Avenue
Chicago, IL 60601

Sales and Marketing Executives International
Student Education Division
630 Third Avenue
New York, NY 10017

Theadore M. Pryor
Pension Planner

Theadore M. Pryor is pension planning underwriter for Aetna Life and Casualty in Hartford, Connecticut. He designs group pension plans for individual employers based on budget, size of company and data provided by field agents. He also develops contract specifications and assures correctness of contract language.

While group pension underwriting is a relatively new and little known activity of the insurance industry, Mr. Pryor feels that the field is "wide open" for blacks and that opportunities "should increase in this and related fields with the passage of federal pension legislation." He is a retired United States Army master

sergeant.

Mr. Pryor was born July 27, 1932 in New Orleans, Louisiana. He has a B.S. degree in economics from Central Connecticut State College (1965). He and his wife Sophornia have four children: Zylpha, Tedra, Delstwirtz and Jajul. He is an advocate of black businesses "expanding their points of reference to national and international frameworks." In 1972, he staged the first national black trade show. Among the 120 exhibitors were twenty-three black manufacturing firms.

Career Information

Training

An underwriter assesses the acceptability of various types of risks by analyzing information—in the case of the pension planning underwriter, on a company's size and its budget. College graduates are sought for entry-level positions in underwriting. Employers look for candidates with a liberal arts or business administration degree, although a major in almost any college field provides a good general background. A beginning underwriter usually goes through a company-sponsored training program and sometimes supplements on-the-job training by home study courses, instruction at home-office schools or at local colleges and universities. This supplemental training enhances advancement opportunities.

Outlook

The need for underwriters throughout the remainder of the decade is listed as only moderate. Expansion in the field depends upon population increases and growth in the work force.

Additional Source Material

Institute of Life Insurance
277 Park Avenue
New York, NY 10017

Insurance Information Institute
110 William Street
New York, NY 10038

American Mutual Insurance Alliance
20 N. Wacker Drive
Chicago, IL 60606

Rick Ratcliffe

Manager, Technical Studies

Rick Ratcliffe manages the technical studies group for Audio Magnetic corporation, a Mattel subsidiary. The group conducts research on mechanical performance of tape cassettes and cartridges with the ultimate goal of developing superior products.

With fifteen years experience in the aerospace testing service, and three years in Mattel's Research and Development Division as a staff engineer, Mr. Ratcliffe achieved his present managerial status as a result of Mattel's policy of drawing on the corporate talent pool afforded by all its subsidiaries. He knows of few blacks in non-aerospace private industry in his field, but thinks that opportunities should be excellent in companies small enough "for your voice to be heard. It is difficult to make your value known in a large company if you [a black] start off at the bottom of the ladder . . ."

Mr. Ratcliffe went to the University of California at Los Angeles (B.A. in physics, 1951; M.S. in engineering, 1963; Ph.D. in engineering, 1970), where his studies concentrated on control systems, mechanical dynamics and mathematics. He has developed an automatic photographic recording system for Optigan Corporation, another Mattel subsidiary, and has worked on an explosive condition warning and prevention system for a Cleveland company before joining Mattel.

146

Rick Ratcliffe was born in St. Louis, Missouri, on October 21, 1928, is married to Dolores Corita Ratcliffe, and enjoys movies, sports, music, art and literature in his spare time.

Career Information

Training
Technical positions run the educational requirement gamut from on-the-job training to a Ph.D. in the appropriate field. Before the rise to an engineering research management position, the candidate should have a bachelor's degree (a bachelor's at entry level usually qualifies the student for research assistantships). Advancement depends on experience and additional study in the field. Entry at a level of high research responsibility requires an advanced degree. The requisite management skills arise from on-the-job experience or from courses taken as a college undergraduate, company-sponsored training institutes or from local colleges or universities (see *Training* under other managerial occupations).

Outlook
Employment opportunities for engineers are expected to be favorable through the 1970s. Engineers who are not well-grounded in fundamentals and whose specialization is very narrow could be affected adversely by shifts in defense activities and rapidly changing technology.

Additional Source Material
National Society of Professional Engineers
2029 K Street, NW
Washington, DC 20006

Engineering Manpower Commission
Engineers Joint Council
345 E. 47th Street
New York, NY 10017

Hugh A. Robertson

Director, Film Editor

Hugh A. Robertson is a feature film editor and director. Most recently, he directed the film *Melinda*, starring Calvin Lockhart, Rosalind Cash and Vonetta McGee. He was the editor of *Shaft* and was nominated for an Academy Award for his editing of the movie *Midnight Cowboy*.

Robertson has worked over twenty years in the film industry on both coasts in film editing, the process of putting together a movie by artistically cutting and splicing the many feet of film that have been shot. Initially a movie-can carrier for Seaboard Studios in New York, Robertson entered the Motion Picture and Television Institute in Brooklyn, later applying that training to a job as filmmaker in the Army Signal Corps.

Through the intervention of an employer, film editor Carl Lerner, Robertson was admitted to the motion picture editors' union eleven years after his first application. He went on to serve as assistant editor on *12 Angry Men*, *Patterns*, *The Miracle Worker*, *Lilith* and others.

In spite of obstacles and frustrations, Robertson remained in the industry, he says, "because I honestly enjoy working with film. It's a personal fulfillment. A filmmaker is, after all, an artist." He advises young blacks thinking of a career in filmmaking to seek training at the University of California at Los Angeles or the University of Southern California. Opportunities for blacks are opening, he feels, especially with the advent of the new black movies.

Career Information

Training

There are no specific training requirements for entry into the film industry, but increasingly colleges and universities, technical schools and specialized communications schools are offering degrees in filmmaking, editing, sound application and other areas in the visual arts. These schools offer excellent preparation for entry-level positions. Because of the large numbers of young people interested in the visual arts, those with specialized backgrounds may find starting positions more easily.

Outlook

The film industry has undergone drastic changes in recent years. Large studios employing thousands have reduced operations in an answer to changing public tastes. The trend is toward independent production and smaller operation. Even though this is the case, many young people are attracted to this phase of the visual arts, and competition is very rigorous for the few openings available each year. Those with a strong background in theory, method and visual mechanics stand a better chance.

Additional Source Material

The American Film Institute
501 Doheny Road
Beverley Hills, CA 90210

Frank W. Roselle Jr.

Recruitment Director

Frank W. Roselle Jr. is director of recruitment at Mattel, Inc. in Hawthorne, California. With a staff of seven, he oversees the recruitment of corporate personnel ranging from executives and other professionals to clerical staff for such departments as marketing, engineering, administration, systems and finance. Previously, he was manager of recruitment projects and manager of marketing recruitment. Mr. Roselle, who was born April 7, 1937 in Greenwich, Connecticut, has a B.A. degree in economics from Iona College in New Rochelle, New York. On-the-job training, he says, has provided him with an understanding of business and corporate organization. The number of blacks at his level is low in large corporations, and opportunities for blacks in manufacturing are very good, he believes.

Mr. Roselle is president of the Mattel Federal Credit Union and vice president of the Mattel Management Association. He and his wife, Linda, and their four children live in Inglewood, California where he is a commissioner of the Civil Service Review Board. His leisure interests include sports, reading, music and theater.

Career Information

Training
Personnel recruitment may cover the entire range of a company's employee needs. An undergraduate degree in personnel or business administration fits the applicant very well for entry-level positions in this field. Holders of degrees in other areas such as office management and industrial relations may, with some on-the-job training or training from a company institute or an outside college or university, eventually assume a recruitment position. Training requirements also depend largely on the nature of the place of employment.

Outlook
College graduates who enter personnel work may expect to find ample positions through the 1970s. Although employment prospects probably will be best for those who have specialized training in personnel administration, positions will be available for those with degrees in other fields.

Additional Source Material
American Society for Personnel Administration
19 Church Street
Berea, OH 44017

Clovis E. Scott
Inspection Supervisor

Clovis E. Scott supervises eleven aircraft plumbing and electrical
inspectors at Lockheed Aircraft (California Division) in Palmdale,
California. He is responsible for the inspection of all newly designed
plumbing and electrical parts and all subcontracted parts from
suppliers.

     Mr. Scott studied industrial tool design for one year at Los Angeles
Valley College and attended the Lockheed Management Institute at the
University of Southern California. He has also taken a course for
supervisors sponsored by Lockheed. Previously, he taught
special courses at Lockheed's Watts-Willowbrook Plant where a

152

number of young blacks are employed. He is a member of his company's Affirmative Action Board. He believes that future opportunities are good for blacks in his field.

Mr. Scott was born March 31, 1924 in Topeka, Kansas. He and his wife, Theodora, have four children: Darrell, Clovis, Durand and Torin. They live in Pacoima, California. In his leisure time, Mr. Scott breeds and trains horses. He has a brown belt in judo and a first-degree black belt in ju-jitsu.

Career Information

Training
Beginning jobs in inspection require no college training. Those with experience and aptitude may rise through the ranks to become foremen and supervisors. For entry purposes, however, inspectors generally are trained on the job for a period of time. The extent of training depends on the nature of the job. Employers may hire applicants who do not have a high school diploma but have qualifying aptitudes or related experience. Some employers prefer experienced production workers for inspection jobs. Courses offered in technical schools, such as blueprint reading and shop mathematics, enhance advancement possibilities.

Outlook
Employment of inspectors is expected to increase only moderately through the 1970s. Most of the openings will arise as a result of normal occupational shifts. The growing complexity of manufactured products should also result in the need for more inspectors; however, increasing use of mechanized and automatic inspection equipment will partially offset this factor.

Additional Source Material
(The following addresses pertain to careers in the aircraft, missile and spacecraft industry. For information about inspection occupations in other fields, contact your local office of the state employment service.)

International Association of Machinists
   and Aerospace Workers
1300 Connecticut Avenue, NW
Washington, DC 20036

International Union, United Automobile,
   Aerospace and Agricultural Implement
   Workers of America
8000 E. Jefferson Avenue
Detroit, MI 48214

Ramon S. Scruggs Sr.
Director of Minority Affairs

Ramon S. Scruggs Sr. is director of minority affairs at American Telephone & Telegraph Company in New York, New York. His is a position that he proposed to AT&T—one that would be, he advised, "a symbol to minority employees and to the minority communities, particularly black and Spanish, of this company's interest in matters which concern them both." His work involves employment problems of minorities as well as AT&T's participation in community affairs that affect minority customers.

Mr. Scruggs began his career with the Bell System in 1939 as a commercial agent with Michigan Bell in Detroit, Michigan. He was the company's first black employee ("Not even a black cleaning woman or elevator operator was among the 4,000 employees in the building," he recalls).

Born February 19, 1909 in Nashville, Tennessee, Mr. Scruggs has an A.B. degree in business administration from Fisk University. He has honorary LL.D. degrees from Central Michigan University and Bishop College. He is a trustee of Fisk and of Hampton Institute.

154

Mr. Scruggs believes that opportunities will increase in the communications industry. "My objective is to have blacks, Spanish persons and other minorities working at all jobs at all levels," he says. He has a daughter, Mrs. Marie L. Inniss, and a son, Ramon Jr. He and his wife, Helen, live in Newark, New Jersey.

Career Information

Training
Minority affairs and affirmative action directorships are an outgrowth of government regulations against employment discrimination. Preparation for such upper-level management positions is the same as that for all management positions—most employers seek applicants with a college degree. The degree areas stressed are business administration, accounting, economics or finance. Managerial skills can be applied as effectively in one job as the next; all that is required is orientation to that particular company's operating procedures. Once an entry-level position is obtained, advancement comes with demonstrated competence, experience and additional study such as that offered by company training institutes, private organizations, and local colleges or universities.

Outlook
The managerial outlook in general is expected to remain good throughout the 1970s. The survival of positions in minority affairs and affirmative action depends on the continuation of government legislation and monitoring, and the commitment of individual industries to equal opportunity practices.

Additional Source Material
The American Management Association
135 W. 50th Street
New York, NY 10020

Charles Clifford Shockley III
Executive Pilot

Charles Clifford Shockley III is an executive pilot and senior captain employed by Philip Morris, Inc. Based in New York, New York, he flies key executives of the company on domestic and international flights. His plane is a Grumman Gulfstream. He obtained the job through the New York Urban League.

Mr. Shockley was born February 10, 1938 in Camden, New Jersey. He has a B.S. degree in biology from Virginia State College (1961). He was an aviator in the United States Army for seven years, and graduated from the U. S. Army Fixed Wing Aviation School. He also completed the infantry advanced course—a course which "gave me insight into aviation needs of the army and foreign armies at all levels." He also has an airline transport rating, the highest-level pilot's license obtainable. He is a member of Omega Psi Phi fraternity and Negro Airmen's International Association.

Mr. Shockley urges qualified black pilots to send a resume to the New York Urban League. "There are openings now available," he says. Divorced, he has two children, Charles IV and Karen. He enjoys bowling and teaching in an adult tutoring program.

Career Information

Training
Persons interested in piloting may receive training through military service or a private flying school. Federal Aviation Administration requirements vary with the type of license sought by the pilot. The airline transport license (that required of "captains" on commercial air lines) requires at least 1,500 hours flying time within the previous eight years including night and instrument flying time.

Outlook
Employment of pilots in general aviation activities is expected to grow very rapidly, particularly in business flying, aerial application, air-taxi operations and patrol and survey flying.

Additional Source Material
Air Line Pilots Association, International
1329 E Street, NW
Washington, DC 20004

Samuel Simmons

Market Developer

Samuel Simmons is national market development manager at Sunshine Biscuits, Inc., in New York, New York. He is responsible for development of sales as well as marketing and advertising programs in

all principal United States markets for the manufacture of crackers, cookies and other snack products. Previously, he was a local market manager and regional manager for the Great Lakes Area.

Opportunities in his industry are unlimited for blacks, Mr. Simmons believes. His job has made him aware of the tremendous impact and buying power of blacks for all corporations in America.

Born May 23, 1927 in Chicago, Illinois, Mr. Simmons attended Roosevelt University in Chicago and Triton College in River Grove, Illinois. He and his wife, June, have a daughter, Fern Patrice. They live in Scotch Plains, New Jersey.

Mr. Simmons urges other blacks to consider food industry careers "because this industry will always be needed."

Career Information

Training

In the field of sales and marketing, there are countless subfields, most of which require similar educational backgrounds at the entry level, with specialization coming after some experience with a particular company and a firm grounding in that company's operating procedures. A market developer must combine a good sense for the marketing of a company's existing products or services with an intuition for feeling out new markets and the products that will appeal to them. The best preparation is a degree in business administration, marketing or management. Methods of statistical analysis are also becoming an educational requisite.

Outlook

College graduates trained in marketing research and statistics are likely to find favorable job opportunities throughout the 1970s. The growing complexity of United States markets and consumer trends will also expand possibilities for psychologists, economists and other social scientists. Holders of masters degrees and doctorates will find the outlook excellent.

Additional Source Material
American Marketing Association
230 North Michigan Avenue
Chicago, IL 60601

Sales and Marketing Executives International
Student Education Division
630 Third Avenue
New York, NY 10017

Robert Small

Publications Director

Robert Small is staff director for the American Bar Association Press in Chicago, Illinois. He supervises the preparation of hundreds of newsletters, journals, posters and slides, and the association's annual report.

Recruited from *Current Anthropology* magazine where he held a production position, Mr. Small has taken courses in graphic presentation at the Illinois Printing Institute. He is also a member of the Chicago Book Clinic and a judge for the clinic's annual book show honoring excellence in design, typography and overall book production.

160

According to Mr. Small, "the door has swung open" as far as the editorial aspects of publishing are concerned, and the growth in all areas of graphic arts has created unlimited opportunities. Inroads still remain to be made in the manufacturing end, however, Mr. Small said.

Born December 20, 1933, in Kansas City, Missouri, Mr. Small has been a professional actor. He is single and lives in Chicago.

Career Information

Training

About four thousand schools—high schools, vocational schools, technical institutes and colleges—offer courses in printing and graphic arts. As with all jobs, a managerial position, if not trained for directly, is achieved after some years of experience in the field. Any supervisory slot requires a thorough knowledge of the field, and the best way to prepare is with a theoretical basis from an accredited institution. If entry is desired at the managerial level, the requisite managerial training (discussed elsewhere in this book) is suggested along with courses in the desired field and, in most cases, additional on-the-job instruction.

Outlook

Some employment increase in new types of jobs will result from technological changes in production methods. Concomitantly, more managers will be required for supervision of new publications and with expertise in coordinating the appropriate production methods with the needs of the printing job.

Additional Source Material

Education Council of the
   Graphic Arts Industry, Inc.
4615 Forbes Avenue
Pittsburgh, Pa 15213

Printing Industries of America, Inc.
1730 North Lynn Street
Arlington, VA 22209

161

William D. Stubblefield
Marketing Planning Manager

William D. Stubblefield is marketing planning manager at American
Health Facilities, Inc., a subsidiary of American Hospital Supply
Corporation, in Winnetka, Illinois. He assesses opportunities for
expansion and refinement of the company's services, and examines the
organizational, financial, legal and staffing problems involved in
meeting market needs. He also reviews the results of advertising
campaigns, and sets standards and guidelines to follow in determining
the effectiveness of advertising.

Mr. Stubblefield is a graduate of the University of Dubuque (Iowa). He has taken post-graduate business courses and participated in a management and training program at AHSC. Prior to joining the firm, he was a captain in the United States Army Intelligence Corps, and served in Europe and in Vietnam.

"There is an abundance of talented blacks in marketing," he says. "Unfortunately, there has been a tendency to assign them to 'special' markets rather than the mainstream jobs. Opportunities for blacks in marketing and finance are good," he says, and "the corporate need for innovative programs and new products is increasingly overriding any desire to exclude minorities from professional opportunities."

Mr. Stubblefield and his wife, Alice, have a daughter, Angela. They live in Chicago, Illinois. He is interested in chess, jazz and classical music, tennis and photography.

Career Information

Training
Marketing planning is a response to the need for companies to make significant and accurate choices for the most efficient marketing of their goods and services. Therefore, people interested in this field are best prepared with a degree in business administration, marketing or management. The same position in a small company may also require some knowledge of personnel and commercial law. Methods of statistical analysis are also becoming an educational requisite.

Outlook
College graduates trained in marketing research and statistics are likely to find favorable job opportunities throughout the decade. The growing complexity of marketing research techniques will also expand opportunities for psychologists, economists and other social scientists. Applicants with masters degrees and doctorates will find the outlook excellent.

Additional Source Material
American Marketing Association
230 North Michigan Avenue
Chicago, IL 60601

Willi Sturkey

Executive Secretary

Willi Sturkey is executive secretary to the vice president and general counsel of American Motors Corporation in Detroit, Michigan. ''It is impossible'', she says, ''to list all of the duties of an executive secretary, but if you include all the prerequisites listed in a secretarial manual and multiply them by five, you probably have an accurate description.''

Mrs. Sturkey, who was born August 6, 1926 in Chicago, Illinois, joined American Motors in 1963, following referral from an employment agency. Her first job, while attending high school and college, was with a well-known dermatologist, the late Dr. Theodore K. Lawless of Chicago, Illinois. Later she was an editorial secretary at Johnson Publishing Company in Chicago. She was promoted to her present position in 1972 when she was chosen by AMC's newly-elected vice president and general counsel.

Mrs. Sturkey attended Roosevelt University in Chicago, Victory Business College, Wayne State University and the University of Detroit. She believes that future opportunities for blacks as executive secretaries are "unlimited for the untiring worker."

She and her husband, Harold, have two children, Harold Jr. and Sherrian. Her hobbies include golf, reading, bridge and pinochle.

Career Information

Training

The position of executive secretary requires a considerable range of office management skills. The executive secretary must be fully capable of handling the specialized duties peculiar to the company by which he or she is employed. Capable and well-trained stenographers and secretaries have excellent opportunities for advancement. Both may eventually be promoted to jobs such as administrative assistant, office supervisor, executive secretary or some other responsible position requiring specialized knowledge. Training for these low-level entry positions includes a high school diploma and study in business and office practice, shorthand and typing. However, there are bachelor's degrees conferred by schools of business and commerce in many universities, and some even offer a master's. As with any job where the skill pool is becoming increasingly demanding, those with a college background have improved possibilities for entry and advancement.

Outlook

Employment opportunities are expected to be favorable for the remainder of the decade. Most new positions are created by the rapid turnover in the profession.

Additional Source Material

United Business Schools Association
1730 M Street, NW
Washington, DC 20036

The Institute for Certifying Secretaries
616 E. 63rd Street
Kansas City, MO 64110

Barbara Jo Taylor
Food Product Supervisor

Barbara Jo Taylor is a product group supervisor employed by the Betty Crocker Division of General Mills, Inc. She supervises two test kitchens and a staff of four home economists responsible for the creation, development and testing of food products and recipes.

Prior to her present position, Miss Taylor was a test kitchen home economist with Betty Crocker. She holds a bachelor of science degree in dietetics from the University of Northern Colorado.

As a little girl, Barbara Jo thought it would be exciting to be a Betty Crocker home economist. One of the most satisfactory experiences in her career has been teaching dietary management to wives of heart patients during a General Mills-sponsored nutrition research project. She initiated a series of classes in how to make special diets attractive, interesting, and workable.

Miss Taylor knows of no other major food company which has a black test-kitchen supervisor and considers future opportunities in this field excellent.

In leisure moments, Miss Taylor enjoys fashion, sewing, theater, baseball and reading. She is unmarried.

Career Information

Training

The minimum educational requirement for dietitians is a bachelor's degree with a major in foods and nutrition or institution management. This degree is obtainable from about 400 colleges and universities. Undergraduate work should include courses in foods and nutrition, institution management, chemistry, bacteriology, and physiology and related courses such as mathematics, psychology, sociology and economics. Such preparation is necessary when the position requires development and testing of new food products. A knowledge of government standards is also required.

Outlook

Opportunities for qualified dietitians are expected to be very good in the coming years. An increasing number will be needed to direct food services for hospitals, schools, industrial plants and commercial eating places, and to engage in food and nutrition research programs.

Additional Source Material
The American Dietetic Association
620 North Michigan Avenue
Chicago, IL 60611

Comer L. Taylor Jr.

Regional Planner

Comer L. Taylor Jr. is a regional planner with the Tennessee Valley Authority, Knoxville, Tennessee. He assists TVA communities in planning industrial site locations and in solving or reducing overall development problems.

Mr. Taylor earned both his bachelor's and master's degrees in planning in four years at Alabama Agricultural and Mechanical University, Normal, Alabama, where he maintained an A-average. In spite of the small number of blacks in the field, Taylor considers the government funds offered to blacks entering planning an indication of good future opportunities.

Mr. Taylor was born October 12, 1949, in Fort Lauderdale, Florida. He and his wife, Crystal have one daughter, Tracy. In his leisure time, Mr. Taylor raises tropical fish and plays touch football.

168

Career Information

Training

Employers consider a master's degree in planning the most desirable educational background for professional work in this field. In federal agencies and a growing number of other government agencies, two years of graduate work or its equivalent is required for most entry-level positions. However, young people having an undergraduate degree in city planning, architecture, landscape architecture, engineering, public administration or another social science field may qualify for entrance level positions. As of this writing, more than fifty schools offered degrees (graduate) in urban planning, a bachelor's degree in one of the above named fields is required for entrance into graduate school.

Outlook

Employment prospects for the well-qualified planner are good for the remainder of the decade. The need for planners will rise as city and regional administrators turn to professionals in matters of industrial and population growth. Construction of new cities and towns is also anticipated to add to the need for planners.

Additional Source Materials

American Institute of Planners
917 15th Street, NW
Washington, DC 20005

American Society of Planning Officials
1313 E. 60th Street
Chicago, IL 60637

169

Joseph H. Tazewell
Chemist, Research Group Leader

Joseph H. Tazewell heads a research group in the Plastics and Fibers
Division of Firestone Tire and Rubber Company in Akron, Ohio. In the
Central Research Laboratory, he supervises four scientists and two
technicians in developing new plastics and synthetic fibers.
He directs the work of three scientists with Ph.D. degrees, even
though he has no doctorate himself. He also conducts an independent
research program at Firestone, a company which grosses
approximately $2.5 billion a year.

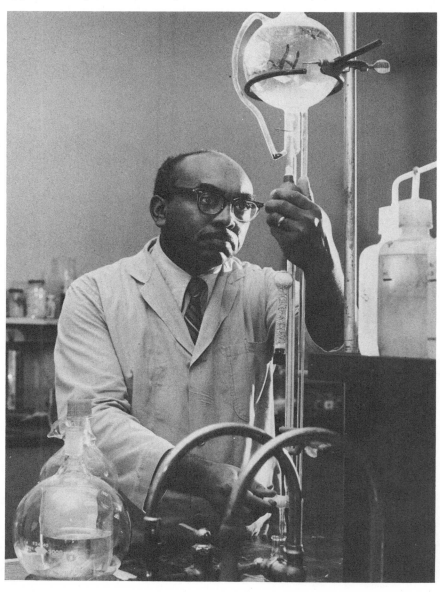

170

Mr. Tazewell is a 1953 graduate (B.S., chemistry) of Hampton Institute. Following graduation, he was granted a Firestone Fellowship to study polymer chemistry at the University of Akron. He joined Firestone in 1954 as a research chemist, then completed management training courses offered by the company. He was promoted after thirteen years as a research chemist. He cites as his most significant achievement the issuance of five United States patents and numerous foreign patents for his work in plastics and synthetic fibers.

Opportunities for blacks he says, "will continue to be good in the multi-disciplined field of polymer science for the foreseeable future."

Born June 1, 1932 in Portsmouth, Virginia, Mr. Tazewell is married and lives in Akron with his wife, Barbara, and four children: Joseph, Jonathan, Paul and Thomas. He is a member of the American Chemical Society, participates in church and community activities, and builds model trains as a hobby.

Career Information

Training
A bachelor's degree with a major in chemistry is usually the minimum educational requirement for starting a career as a chemist. Graduate training is essential for many positions, particularly in research and college teaching, and is helpful for advancement in all types of work. Training leading to a bachelor's degree is offered at about one thousand colleges and universities throughout the United States. In addition to the required courses in analytical, inorganic, organic and physical chemistry, the undergraduate major also takes courses in mathematics (especially analytical geometry and calculus) and physics.

Outlook
The employment outlook is expected to be favorable. Chemists will continue to be needed to conduct research and development work and also to produce new products that result in additional opportunities for scientists in other fields.

Additional Source Material
American Chemical Society
1155 16th Street, NW
Washington, DC 20036

Manufacturing Chemists' Association, Inc.
1825 Connecticut Avenue, NW
Washington, DC 20009

Walter E. Thornton
Goods Superintendent

Walter E. Thornton is finished goods superintendent at Joseph E. Seagram & Sons, Inc. in Louisville, Kentucky. He coordinates the production and shipment of a variety of liquor brands and bottle sizes according to customer needs. He also oversees the entire operation of the Seagram warehouse for finished products, and supervises twenty-eight employees. Previously, he was a research technician, warehouse supervisor, traffic planner and finished goods planner at Seagram. He was promoted after seven years of employment. ''Opportunities are excellent in production management with Seagram for any black who is willing to work diligently toward preparing for job responsibility and challenge,'' he says.

A graduate of Kentucky State University, Mr. Thornton has a B.S. degree in biology. In college, he earned eight varsity letters in sports while maintaining a B-plus average. He was born March 3, 1943 in Gary, West Virginia. He and his wife, Jacqueline, have two children, Kathy and Karen. In his leisure time he coaches Gary-Y Little League football, plays golf and reads seventeenth and eighteenth century poetry.

Career Information

Training

This position combines many of the features of production management and industrial traffic management. Although persons having no more than a high school education can qualify for such a position, the rise to superintendent is based on experience within the company. For entry at a management level, college is required. College courses in business, traffic management, transportation, economics, etc. are good bases for such a position. Workers in traffic departments may advance by participating in company-sponsored training programs, by taking courses in colleges or universities or schools specializing in traffic management or by attending seminars sponsored by private organizations. "Certified" membership in the American Society of Traffic and Transportation, Inc. can be acquired by successfully completing the society's four examinations and meeting certain educational and experience requirements. College credit may be substituted for three of the four examinations.

Outlook

Factors expected to affect the moderate rise in such employment are the increasing emphasis in many industries on efficient management of transportation activities and the trend toward procuring raw materials and finished products from more distant places and distributing them to increasingly wider markets. Efficient handling of storage is also a need to be filled by industry in the future.

Additional Source Material

American Society of Traffic and Transportation, Inc.
22 West Madison Street
Chicago, IL 60602

Richard Louis Van Dyke

Evaluation Specialist

Richard Louis Van Dyke is a senior advanced systems evaluations specialist with International Telephone and Telegraph Company in New York, New York. He coordinates the firm's data collection and the divisional participation for the ITT nationwide computer study. His work includes making on-site surveys and attending regional meetings of data processing managers of the various ITT companies. Mr. Van Dyke prepared for his present work by serving as a technical consultant and as Director of Scientific Marketing for ITT in Brazil. He has taken courses in statistical analysis, systems and programming, and has been an ITT manager dealing with customer applications.

He is a graduate of Wilson Junior College in Chicago, Illinois (associate of science degree) and New York University (B.S. degree in electrical engineering). He is presently studying at NYU for a graduate degree in business administration.

Commenting on opportunities for blacks, Mr. Van Dyke says: "Any noteworthy corporate position is rare for a black. Blacks are in entry level jobs, and occasionally in equal opportunity positions, but seldom in corporate staff decision-making areas." Nevertheless, he says that opportunities for blacks in data processing are excellent.

Showing blacks that "they can make it," Mr. Van Dyke has co-authored a book, *White-Collar Blacks: A Breakthrough?* The book is published by the American Management Association.

Mr. Van Dyke was born September 25, 1938 in Chicago. He and his wife, Sherrilyn, have four children.

Career Information

Training
Systems analysis covers considerable occupational territory, and there is no universally acceptable way to prepare for work in this field. Most employers prefer to hire people who have had some experience in computer programming. A young person can learn to use electronic data-processing equipment on-the-job or he can take courses offered by employers, computer manufacturers or colleges. In large electronic data-processing departments, a person who begins as a junior systems analyst and gains experience may be promoted to senior systems analyst or lead systems analyst. Those having proven leadership ability also can advance to positions as systems analysis managers. Additional managerial skills gained through company programs or outside courses are most helpful for advancement.

Outlook
The employment prospect for systems analysts should be excellent throughout the 1970s. A growing demand for systems analysts will result from the rapid expansion of electronic data-processing systems in business and government. Greater emphasis will be placed on developing computer systems that retrieve information faster, solve complex problems and monitor industrial processes. These developments and others suggest a rapid rise in employment.

Additional Source Material
American Federation of Information
   Processing Societies
210 Summit Avenue
Montvale, NJ 07645

Data Processing Management Association
505 Busse Highway
Park Ridge, IL 60068

Milton Oliver Vassell

Physicist

Milton Oliver Vassell is a physicist on the technical staff of General Telephone & Electronics Laboratories in Waltham, Massachusetts. With a departmental budget of $15 million, he directs research and development in the field of communications. As the resident theorist for a group, he participates in the planning and execution of the group's research program.

Dr. Vassell has been with GTE since 1964. He says that "there are more jobs below the senior level than there are qualified blacks for them." This, he says, "makes the short range forecast extremely favorable."

He has B.S. and Ph.D. degrees in physics from New York University. He was elected to Phi Beta Kappa in 1958, and is a member of Pi Mu Epsilon (mathematics) and Sigma Pi Sigma (physics).

Dr. Vassell was born May 8, 1931 in Kingston, Jamaica. He enjoys golf, bowling and reading in his spare time. He believes that "if one sets high goals at every stage of development and exercises the diligence and patience to achieve them, unsuspected opportunities will present themselves." He and his wife, Dorine, have two children, Karyn and Sheldon.

Career Information

Training

A bachelor's degree with a major in physics is generally the minimum requirement for those seeking careers as physicists. Graduate training, often to the doctoral level, is needed for employment involving research and development responsibility. Physicists having a bachelor's degree qualify for a variety of jobs in applied research in private industry or the federal government, or work as research assistants in college while working toward an advanced degree. Over eight hundred colleges and universities offer degree programs in physics, the undergraduate program offering a broad science background as a basis for graduate or on-the-job specialization.

Outlook

According to the *Occupational Outlook Handbook* published by the U.S. Bureau of Labor Statistics, employment outlooks for the rest of the decade are favorable, but graduate training is increasingly requisite. Through the 1970s, research and development expenditures are expected to increase but at a slower rate than in the 1960s because of reduced importance of space and defense components.

Additional Source Material

American Institute of Physics
335 E. 45th Street
New York, NY 10017

Interagency Board
U. S. Civil Service Examiner
1900 E Street, N. W.
Washington, DC 20415

Robert M. Waite

Assistant Product Line Manager

Robert M. Waite is assistant product line manager-natural resources at International Telephone and Telegraph Corporation in New York, New York. He plans and manages ITT's natural resource companies, including those involved in mining, wood products, paper products, chemical cellulose and wood chemicals. Some 350 persons are under Mr. Waite's supervision. Previously, he was a natural resources planning manager at ITT, the ninth largest corporation in the United States.

Born September 14, 1928 in Freetown, Sierra Leone, West Africa, Mr. Waite has a B.S. degree in economics from Case-Western Reserve

University in Cleveland, Ohio and an M.B.A. degree in management and finance from New York University. He believes that the field of natural resources and environmental planning offers excellent opportunities for blacks. He considers his most significant achievement the building of the first radio factory on the West Coast of Africa. He once was managing director of Nigerian Electronics and still serves as director of Maiden Electronics, Ltd. in Lagos, Nigeria. He is a past national director of the Interracial Council for Business Opportunity.

Mr. Waite and his wife, Joan, have three children: Robin, Monty and Robert. They live in Teaneck, New Jersey.

Career Information

Training

Any position dealing with natural resources requires a scientific background, and entry into a natural resource management position can be made from the technical perspective or from the managerial. For entry that will eventually lead to a managerial position, the applicant should have college training with at least a bachelor's degree. Professional workers usually start at a junior level in field research, and with experience move into administrative positions. Scientists and engineers having research ability, preferably those with advanced degrees, may transfer more easily to management positions. From the managerial standpoint, beginning managers do much better with a college degree in business administration, finance, accounting or economics. On-the-job technical training and experience eventually lead to top level management positions.

Outlook

Natural resource and environmental research is expanding rapidly and will, therefore require many more qualified scientists. Those with at least a college degree will find entry positions more easily than others. Management positions are expected to continue at a favorable level throughout the remainder of the decade. Again, employers favor those with college training as management trainees.

Additional Source Material

American Institute of Biological Sciences
3900 Wisconsin Avenue, NW
Washington, DC 20016

Ecological Society of America
Connecticut College
New London, CT 06320

James Watkins
Shop Foreman, Electronic Assembly

James Watkins is a departmental shop foreman in electronic assembly for General Telephone and Electronics' Automatic Electric Company in Northlake, Illinois. He supervises 118 people in the production of electronic printed wiring cards used on equipment made at GTE. Employed by the company for nineteen years and in his present position for seven, Mr. Watkins was upgraded from his first job as a bench worker to group leader and then to his management responsibilities. He received on-the-job training and also spent four years with the University of Illinois management development program.

Mr. Watkins believes that the position which he holds is not a rarity and that "any steady working, ambitious, trainable black can reach this job level. Opportunities for blacks are unlimited," he says, "but blacks must raise their heads and say "I am ready."

Mr. Watkins played for seven years with the Harlem Globetrotters and four years with the Chicago Brown Bombers basketball team. Still a sports buff, he now officiates at local basketball and softball games in his spare time. He and his wife, Elizabeth, have two sons and a daughter.

Career Information

Training
Foreman positions are among the few that do not require a college background of any sort. Rather, they call for years of experience within a company and a rise through production ranks. Foremen do have a thorough grounding in all phases of the production procedure. With the high degree of specialization in modern industries, some employers are hiring trainees with foreman positions in mind, and these are usually college graduates. Courses in management offered by the firm or through colleges and universities are a great aid in enhancing advancement possibilities.

Outlook
The number of foremen to be employed in manufacturing industries throughout the seventies is expected to grow only moderately. There will, however, be a rapid increase in the number of foremen needed in non-manufacturing industries—such as construction, trade, service and public utilities.

Additional Source Material
American Management Association
135 W. 50th Street
New York, NY 10020

Charles F. Williams Jr.

Vice President Quality Assurance

Charles F. Williams is vice president-product safety and quality assurance at Mattel, Inc., in Hawthorne, California. He is responsible for the safety, durability and reliability of all Mattel toys and products. He supervises 320 employees at the firm which has sales of $275 million a year. Other positions he has held at Mattel include chemical engineer and manager of the quality control department. He joined the firm in 1962.

A graduate of Western Michigan University, Mr. Williams has B.S. degrees in biology, mathematics, chemistry and physics. He also has done graduate work at Massachusetts Institute of Technology.

Aside from being elected as a vice president of the world's largest manufacturer of toys, he considers his greatest achievement is having been selected as chief delegate from the

United States to the International Electrotechnical Commission which met in 1972 in Athens, Greece. He is a member of several organizations, including the American Association for the Advancement of Science, the Industry Advisory Council of Underwriters' Laboratories and the American Society for Quality Control.

He and his wife, Jean, have a daughter, Mrs. Rebecca Hammons, and three sons, Eric, Kim, and Kevin. Deep sea fishing, yachting and traveling are among Mr. Williams' leisure interests.

Career Information

Training
Because quality assurance involves bacteriological, chemical and physical tests on raw components and the finished product, people involved in the field need firm backgrounds in analytical phases of the sciences. Most employers prefer workers who have had some form of specialized training for the more responsible technician positions. Specialized formal training programs are offered in post-secondary schools, technical institutes, junior and community colleges, and technical divisions of four-year colleges. Advancement within the field to a position of responsibility such as vice president requires distinguished service on the job, and, in some cases, management training.

Outlook
Positions for quality assurance technicians are likely to be good in the coming years because of the demand for compliance with federal standards and the increased activities of consumer groups that demand accountability by industry. Opportunities favor those with specialized training.

Additional Source Material
National Council of Technical Schools
1835 K street, NW
Washington, DC 20006

Engineers' Council for Professional Development
345 E. 47th Street
New York, NY 10017

Careers
and Resources

Scholarships and Financial Aid

Choosing a college is one thing, but guaranteeing sufficient funds for the college of your choice is quite another. A college education is increasingly indispensable but, at the same time, costs are increasing so rapidly that college appears out of reach to many worthy students. This need not be the case. Financial aid programs are available at almost every college and university; scholarship and loan programs, work study projects, and a host of other possibilities are open to any student with the initiative and resources to seek them out. Each school gives details of those programs that it administers in its admissions catalogue. Further information can be obtained by writing to the college admissions director. Scholarships are usually limited to those in financial need and to those who are in the upper academic bracket. To help students who may not have ready access to source material, we have compiled a list of available scholarship aid. We have given information as complete as could be found; in those cases where questions remain, it is recommended that the student write to the appropriate address.

In addition to state aid, and to grants available as guaranteed loans, money is available from religious denominations, labor organizations, and through the American Legion. A letter to the national headquarters of a church group, or to a local labor group, may bring news of available funds that can make a university education a reality for you. The American Legion publishes a guide, *Need a Lift*, to which we are indebted for much of the information in this section, and which is excellent in listing many scholarships available from sources outside the colleges. It can be ordered for 25 cents from The American Legion, Education and Scholarships Program, P.O. Box 1055, Indianapolis, IN 46306. We are also grateful to Project 75, 1020 S. Wabash Avenue, Chicago, IL 60605, for advice in compiling this information. Guaranteed loan information, and where to apply for it, has been listed under *State Aid* in this section. For a student whose family's adjusted income is under $15,000, the government will pay interest up to 7 percent on a loan during school and periods of authorized deferment. If the family income is $15,000 or more, a guaranteed loan may be obtained, but the entire interest must be repaid, up to 7 percent, from the start. Repayment of the principal is not required until at least nine months after completing the course of study, or leaving school. The repayment period for college or graduate school loan may be extended, in some cases, as long as ten years. If the student serves in the armed forces, Peace Corps, VISTA, or returns to school as a full-time student, the repayment period may be deferred. The amount of each loan is arranged between the student and the lending institution. Students should discuss loan possibilities with their banks, savings and loan institutions, credit unions or other lender, or with the financial officer at their school. Inquiry should be made of the individual lending institution as to its eligibility for this guaranteed loan program.

General Aid

The following scholarships carry no eligibility restrictions.

Alpha Phi Alpha
Scholarship awards of $300 to $500 are available to high school seniors. These awards are renewable for four years.

Write to
Alpha Phi Alpha Educational Foundation, Inc.
4778 Lakewood Rd.
Ravenna, OH 44266

American Leaders Foundation
Amounts vary according to individual need. Student must have at least one year of college and not be over 28.

Write to
American Leaders Foundation
c/o Northwestern Pennsylvania Bank
and Trust Co., P.O. Box 037
Scranton, PA 8501

Elks National Foundation Scholarships
Annually, the Elks Foundation of the Imperial Benevolent and Protective Order of Elks of the World grants student awards from $800 to $1,500. High school seniors and college undergraduates are eligible.

Write to
Elks National Foundation Scholarships
Mr. John F. Malley
40 Court Street
Boston, MA 02108

General Motors Corporation
Any high school senior is eligible to apply for GM scholarships. The awards range from $200 to $2,000 (depending on need) and are renewable.

187

Write to
General Motors Corporation
8163 G.M. Building
Detroit, MI 48202

Minority Groups Scholarship Program
Available through the Rockefeller Foundation, these scholarships are open to any high school student applying to one of the following seven colleges.

Write to

Antioch College
Yellow Springs, OH 45387

Reed College
Portland, OR 97202

Carleton College
Northfield, MN 55057

Occidental College
Los Angeles, CA 90041

Grinnell College
Grinnell, IA 50112

Swarthmore College
Swarthmore, PA 19081

Oberlin College
Oberlin, OH 44074

National Achievement Scholarships Program for Outstanding Negro Students
The program offers four-year scholarships ranging from $1,000 to $6,000 to high school seniors for use at the schools of their choice. Candidates must take the National Merit Scholarship Qualifying Test (NMSQT).

Write to
National Achievement Scholarship Program for
Outstanding Negro Students
990 Grove Street
Evanston, IL 60201

The National Commission for Cooperative Education
For engineering, liberal arts, business administration, education, pharmacy, and nursing.

Write to
The National Merit Scholarship Corporation
990 Grove Street
Evanston, IL 60201

RCA
National Merit Scholarship Program

For biomedical engineering, science engineering, industrial relations, dramatic arts, music, etc. Students must qualify on the basis of the NMSQT (see above) and the Scholastic Aptitude Test (SAT). These tests are administered at the students' respective high schools. Winners are given up to $1,500 per year (according to need) and may attend the colleges of their choice.

Write to
National Merit Scholarship Corporation
990 Grove Street
Evanston, IL. 60201

Radio Corporation of America
These awards are administered through individual educational institutions and are offered in a number of fields. Each award is $800 (renewable). Additional information is available through college admissions offices.

United Negro College Fund
Available to high school seniors and college undergraduates for use at any of the forty member-colleges of the Fund. Application may be made through the admissions officer of the respective college, or:

Write to
United Negro College Fund
55 E. 52nd Street
New York, NY 10022

Government Aid Programs

In this category are listed a limited number of scholarships and fellowships offered through governmental agencies.

Title II of the Social Security Act
The act extends support to unmarried sons and daughters of a deceased, disabled or retired parent who continue their education full-time at accredited schools. Information is available at your local Social Security Administration Office.

Public Law 91-230, Part D
The U. S. Commissioner of Education makes grants to institutions of higher education for the training of personnel to work with handicapped children. College juniors, seniors and graduates are eligible. Tuition

189

and fees are paid for all except the junior level awards. The stipends are offered as follows: junior year, $300; senior year, $800; master's level, $2,200; post-master's, $3,200. An allowance of $600 is offered for each dependent of a graduate fellow.

Write to
Director, Division of Training Programs
Bureau of Education for the Handicapped
U. S. Office of Education
Washington, DC 20202

Vocational Rehabilitation Programs
Assistance is extended to disabled persons. Includes counseling and guidance, medical examinations and needed restorative services, training and other services.

Write to
National Rehabilitation Counseling Service
1522 K Street
Washington, DC 20005

Higher Education Personnel Fellowships
Grants are made to colleges and universities to assist them in training teachers, administrators or education specialists. Priority is extended to programs to prepare personnel for junior colleges and for work with the disadvantaged at colleges and universities.

Write to
Division of University Programs
Bureau of Higher Education
U.S. Department of Health, Education and Welfare
Washington, DC 20202

The National Defense Student Loan Program
Each year, this program provides loans totaling close to $100 million to full-time students in colleges or universities (two to four year institutions) who need help and are eligible. Loans are repayable within ten years after graduation; 50 percent is forgiven if the graduate goes into teaching. Students should apply directly to the college they intend to enter, not to the federal government. Maximum of $1,000 per year, $5,000 total loans.

Rehabilitation Services Administration

The administration provides teaching and trainee grants to institutions for graduate students in rehabilitation careers. These careers include physical medicine and rehabilitation, dentistry, physical therapy, occupational therapy, speech pathology and audiology, rehabilitation nursing, rehabilitation social work, prosthetics and orthotics, rehabilitation psychology, rehabilitation counseling, recreation for the ill and handicapped, work evaluation and rehabilitation workshop administration, and other specialized fields such as rehabilitation of the blind, deaf and mentally retarded.

Write to

Division of Manpower Training
Rehabilitation Services Administration
U.S. Department of Health, Education and Welfare
Washington, DC 20201

Social and Rehabilitation Service

The U.S. Department of Health, Education and Welfare offers traineeships to institutions for social work education at the master's and doctoral levels. Students should apply directly to the graduate school of social work where they are currently enrolled, or when applying for admission.

National Wildlife Federation

The federation and its state affiliates award a limited number of graduate fellowships of $2,000 to $4,000 for study in conservation fields at an accredited institution.

Write to

The Executive Director
National Wildlife Federation
1412 16th Street, N.W.
Washington, DC 20036

National Research Council

The Fellowship Office of the Office of Scientific Personnel at the National Research Council annually prepares a list of major *Fellowship Opportunities and Aids to Advanced Education for United States Citizens* and a selected list of the same for foreign nationals. Copies are available upon request.

Write to
National Research Council
National Academy of Sciences
2101 Constitution Avenue
Washington, DC 20418

State Aid

Every state has both governmental and private sources for its residents. While we include here many programs, it is best for the student to contact his or her counselor or the state boards of education for more comprehensive information. It is also noted that most states extend aid to children of veterans who were killed in, died as a result of, or were disabled from, service in World War I, World War II, Korea or Vietnam. Also eligible are children of those listed as prisoners of war or as missing in action. Contact state offices of veterans affairs or the Veterans Administration.
See p. 242 for additional information on aid for medical and other health-related careers.

Alabama

Alabama Department of Education

Grants are made to needy resident students attending Florence State College, Jacksonville State University, Livingston University and Troy State University who agree to teach at least three years in Alabama elementary schools. The 250 scholarships are divided equally among the schools and do not exceed $100 annually.

Write to
Alabama Department of Education
Montgomery, AL 36104

Tuskegee Institute School of Nursing

Scholarships of $600 are available to resident black men or women accepted at Tuskegee Institute School of Nursing. The student must agree to practice nursing for at least two years in Alabama.

Write to
Tuskegee Institute
Tuskegee, AL 36088

Board of Medical (or Dental) Scholarship Awards
192

Awards up to $8,000 for four years are available to any Alabama resident of good character who has been accepted for study at the Medical College of Alabama, the University of Alabama School of Dentistry or at comparable institutions.

Write to
Board of Medical Scholarship Awards
University Station
1600 8th Avenue, South
Birmingham, AL 35294

or

Board of Dental Scholarship Awards
1919 7th Avenue, South
Birmingham, AL 35233

For information on guaranteed loans, write to: Director of Higher Education, Office of Education, Region IV, 50 Seventh St, NE, Atlanta, GA 30323

Alaska

University of Alaska
The highest-ranking senior in each Alaska high school is eligible for scholarships covering room and board costs for two years.

Write to
Financial Aid Officer
University of Alaska
College, AK 99701

Commissioner of Education
A scholarship whose amount is determined by the Commissioner is available to students attending any institution of higher education in Alaska. Grant is to be applied to tuition, fees, books, or room and board. Students must have been Alaska residents for at least two years.

Write to
Commissioner of Education
State Department of Education, Pouch F
Alaska Office Building
Juneau, AK 99801

Commissioner of Public Safety

193

The department offers a grant or loan of $1,500 per year up to two years to a resident enrolled in a program leading to an associate or baccalaureate degree in the field of law enforcement, law probation and parole, or penology.

Write to
Commissioner of Public Safety
State Capitol, Pouch N
Juneau, AK 99801

For information on guaranteed loans, write to:
United Student Aid Funds, Inc., 845 Third Avenue, New York, NY, 10022

Arizona

Waiver of tuition and, in some cases, funds to meet expenses are offered to Arizona residents recommended by high schools to state universities or junior colleges. Make application through high school or school of choice.

For information on guaranteed loans, write to:
Director of Higher Education, Office of Education,
Region IX, 760 Market Street, San Francisco, CA 94102

Arkansas

For information on guaranteed loans, write to:
Student Loan Guarantee Foundation of Arkansas,
1515 W. Seventh Street, Suite 615, Little Rock,
AR 72202

California

State Scholarship and Loan Commission
More than 9,000 competitive scholarships—tuition and fees—are offered to resident students under thirty (in financial need) at any school in the state accredited by the Western Association of Schools and Colleges. Funds are also applicable to students classified as disadvantaged whose potential for college success is not necessarily identified by conventional means (e.g., Scholastic Aptitude Tests, etc.). Grants are to be initiated primarily at public community colleges.

Write to
State Scholarship and Loan Commission
714 P Street
Sacramento, CA 95814

194

For information on guaranteed loans, write to:
Director of Higher Education, Office of Education, Region IX,
50 Fulton Street, San Francisco, CA 94102

Colorado

Colorado Dental Committee
Grants approximating the difference between resident and non-resident tuition at the student's chosen school, plus a modest travel allowance, are available. These are for the use of Colorado residents at any accredited dental school in the United States.

Write to
Colorado Dental Committee
University of Colorado Medical Center
4200 E. 9th Avenue
Denver, CO 80220

Applications for the following should be made through the financial aids officer at the institution the student wishes to attend.

Minority Teacher Incentive Grant
A maximum grant of $1,000 (based on need) for a year and a summer session is available to resident students of racial and ethnic minority groups who agree to teach in Colorado for two years following completion of education. Funds are renewable.

Colorado Work-Study
Funds are available to provide institutional jobs for resident undergraduate students. Amount is determined by need.

Colorado Student Grant
Amounts to be determined by institution are available to assist students enrolled at state institutions.

For information on guaranteed loans, write to:
Director of Higher Education, Office of Education, Region VIII,
9017 Federal Office Building, 19th and Stout Streets, Denver, CO 80202

Connecticut

Yearly awards of $300 (maximum) are to be used by students at

195

Connecticut state colleges who are preparing to teach. Students should apply directly to the state college.

State Board of Examiners for Nursing

Awards (amount to be determined by board) are extended to students in any accredited school of nursing in Connecticut. Also, financial aid may be granted for graduate study in nursing at recognized schools in or out of the state.

Write to
State Board of Examiners for Nursing
79 Elm Street
Hartford, CT 06115

Commissioner for Higher Education

Scholarships of $100 to $1,000 for full-time use at any school accredited by the Commissioner of Higher Education are available for resident high school seniors in upper half of their classes.

Write to
Commissioner for Higher Education
P. O. Box 1320
Hartford, CT 06115

A legal resident of Connecticut whose educational achievement is restricted by economic, environmental or social disadvantages, and who is enrolled in full-time study at an approved college or university in Connecticut, may apply directly to the financial aid officer at the institution.

For information on guaranteed loans, write to:
Connecticut Student Loan Foundation, 251 Asylum Street,
Hartford, CT 06103

Delaware

University of Delaware

Delaware residents attending the university are eligible for renewable awards of varying amounts, depending on financial need.

Write to
Office of the Director of Financial Aid
University of Delaware
Newark, DE 19711

196

Scholarship Advisory Council

Delaware resident students pursuing courses not available in Delaware state institutions may receive renewable funds of up to $800 per year, depending on need and academic qualifications.

Write to
Scholarship Advisory Council
c/o State Board of Education
Dover, DE 19901

For information on guaranteed loans, write to:
Delaware Higher Education Loan Program, 200 W. Ninth Street,
Wilmington, DE 19801

District of Columbia

For information on guaranteed loans, write to:
Program-Coordinating Unit, 1329 E Street NW,
Washington DC 20004

Florida

Two-year residents of Florida with an adjusted family income of less than $15,000 may apply to the office of financial aid at a college or university in Florida. Schools offer 4 per cent loans for tuition, room and board, and books and supplies. Write directly to school.

Department of Education

Grants from $200 to $1,200 are awarded to two-year residents of Florida with demonstrated exceptional financial need.

Write to
Scholarships and Loans Section
Department of Education
Tallahassee, FL 32304

Division of Mental Health

Florida residents accepted in graduate training programs in the field of psychiatry, clinical psychology, clinical social work or psychiatric nursing may receive $240 per month. (Psychology interns are eligible for $300, and rates for psychiatric residents depend on year level.) Persons must work in approved agencies for one month for each month of grant, or repay with 5 percent interest. Applications may also be made through school's clinical training program director.

197

Write to
Manpower Development Coordinator
Division of Mental Health
200 E. Gaines Street
Tallahassee, FL 32304

Osteopathic Training Office Medical Scholarships
Five-year residents accepted for admission by an approved college of osteopathic medicine, and in need of assistance, may apply for renewable $1,000 awards. Recipient must agree to practice osteopathic medicine for five years in a Florida community in need of a physician.

Write to
Osteopathic Training Office Medical Scholarships
Florida State Board of Health
P. O. Box 210
Jacksonville, FL 32201

For information on guaranteed loans, write to:
Director of Higher Education, Office of Education, Region IV,
50 Seventh Street NE, Atlanta, GA 30323

Georgia

State Medical Education Board
Georgia residents who have been accepted at accredited medical colleges, and have financial need, are eligible for a maximum of $10,000 for four years.

Write to
State Medical Education Board
Room 468
244 Washington Street, S. W.
Atlanta, GA 30334

Regents' scholarships are available to Georgia residents attending institutions in the state system. Applications are made through the director of student aid at the institution selected.

State Scholarship Commission
Georgia residents attending accredited institutions preparing for careers in paramedical, professional or educational fields such as nursing, dentistry, pharmacy, dental hygiene, etc., and who are needy,

198

may apply for amounts to be determined by the commission.

Write to
State Scholarship Commission
P. O. Box 38005
Capitol Hill Station
Atlanta, GA 30334

Georgia citizens attending approved Georgia colleges or universities not in the system may apply to the respective institution for $400 per academic year. Funds are limited to freshmen, sophomores and juniors during 1973–74. Extended to undergraduate students in the following 1973–74 academic year except where study leads to a degree in theology, divinity or religious education.

For information on guaranteed loans, write to:
Georgia Higher Education Assistance Corporation, P.O. Box 38005, Atlanta, GA 30334

Hawaii

High school senior residents of five years wishing to attend one of six community colleges or a four-year college on the island of Hawaii, Hilo College and in Honolulu (Manoa Campus) for undergraduate study may apply to the financial aids at school selected. Amount to be determined by school.

For information on guaranteed loans, write to:
Director of Higher Education, Office of Education, Region X, 50 Fulton St., San Francisco, CA 94102

Idaho

Idaho State University
The university awards $180 per student for use by state residents at Idaho State University. A freshman honorary scholarship is offered to each high school in Idaho. Selection is to be made by the high school principal and is awarded to a top academic student with regard to need, special skills, or outstanding interest and ability in academic areas.

Write to
Idaho State University
Pocatello, ID 83201

Write to the above address for information on Idaho State University

Club Scholarships which are available to graduating seniors who demonstrate good scholarship and outstanding performance in extra-curricular activities. Awards are $185 each.

Under the same Idaho State University provisions, the State Board of Education may waive a limited number of non-resident tuition fees for disadvantaged and deserving students.

University of Idaho
Scholarships of $300 for University of Idaho students for musical activities in band, orchestra and choir. Available to in- and out-of-state students.

Write to
Director of School of Music
University of Idaho
Moscow, ID 83843

University of Idaho
The university offers out-of-state tuition scholarships for non-resident entering freshmen or transfer students who plan to enroll in the College of Mines to study geological engineering, geology, engineering or metallurgical engineering.

Idaho Mining Association Scholarships are offered ($500) for the freshman year. Also included is guaranteed full-time summer employment in the mining industry during college career including the summer prior to freshman enrollment provided a 2.5 average is maintained.

Idaho Mining Memorial Scholarships of $400 to $500 are offered for use in freshman year to entering freshmen only (in- and out-of-state) with good scholastic records who plan to enroll in the College of Mines to study geography, geological engineering, geology, mining engineering or metallurgical engineering.

Write to
Student Financial Aid Service
University of Idaho
Moscow, ID 83843

For information on guaranteed loans, write to:
Director of Higher Education, Office of Education, Region X,
1321 Second Avenue, Seattle, WA 98101

Illinois

Military Service Scholarships
Tuition and fee funds are available for veterans at an Illinois state-supported college or university or a Class 1 junior college.

General Assembly Awards
To determine eligibility for awards (tuition and fees), the student may write directly to the local member of the General Assembly. Recipient must be a resident of the district and selected by a state legislator. Student must also intend to enroll at an Illinois state-supported college or university.

Illinois State Scholarship Commission
The commission selects recipients for the Illinois Monetary Award (Amount of award varies.) Illinois residents are selected on the basis of need and class rank and must attend an approved college or university.

Write to
Illinois State Scholarship Commission
102 Wilmot Road
Deerfield, IL 60015

Government Aid Programs

Write to
Division of Vocational Rehabilitation
623 E. Adams
Springfield, IL 62706

Department of Children and Family Services
The department offers college tuition waiver and maintenance fees to children of needy families.

Write to
Department of Children and Family Services
524 S. 2nd Street
Springfield, IL 62706

Department of Scholarship Services
A special education grant of $500 per year plus tuition is offered to college juniors and seniors attending approved colleges and universities. Recipient must work in field six months for every year of grant.

201

Write to
Department of Scholarship Services
212 E. Monroe
Springfield, IL 62705

Apply through the high school principal for Special Education Teacher awards of tuition and some fees. Recipient must be in upper half of class, intend to teach special education, and enroll in an Illinois state-supported college or university.

Illinois State Scholarship Commission
Commission offers special bilingual education grants in varying amounts.

Write to
Illinois State Scholarship Commission
102 Wilmont Road
Deerfield, IL 60015

See also preceding section (*State Aid*) for vocational rehabilitation programs.

For information about guaranteed loans, write to:
Illinois Guaranteed Loan Program
102 Wilmot Road, P.O. Box 33
Deerfield, IL 60015

Indiana

All of the following awards are available through financial aids officers at Indiana state-supported institutions of higher learning.

Tuition is offered to full-time students who are children of regular paid law enforcement officers and firemen who have been killed in the line of duty. Must attend a state-supported college, university or technical school.

A partial remission of fees is offered to resident students at state supported colleges and universities through State and Merit Scholarships. Basis of award determined by institution.

Merit Scholarships for remission of non-resident tuition charges are available for non-resident students at state-supported universities.

202

State Scholarship Program

State Scholarships of $100 to $1,400 for tuition and fees are set aside for Indiana residents with superior academic merit and potential, and with financial need. Awards are applicable at eligible institutions within Indiana.

Write to
State Scholarship Commission of Indiana
514 State Office Building
100 N. Senate Avenue
Indianapolis, IN 46204

Educational Grant Programs

Write to above address for information on the grants, which are offered to neediest students. Academic requirement is fulfilled by acceptance for admission into college.

For information about guaranteed loans, write to:
Director of Higher Education, Office of Education, Region V,
226 W. Jackson Boulevard, Chicago, IL 60606

Iowa

Division of Special Education

Funds are for the use of persons preparing professionally for education of the handicapped. Assistance is in the form of summer traineeships at the graduate level in approved special education programs.

Write to
Division of Special Education
State Department of Public Instruction
Grimes State Office Building
Des Moines, IA 50319

Iowa State University

Student residents of Iowa entering Iowa State University are eligible for general scholarships and student aid scholarships (renewable in amounts to be determined by institution). Application should be made by March 1. Parents' Confidential Statement is required.

Write to
Coordinator of Student Financial Aids
Iowa State University
Ames, IA 50010

203

University of Northern Iowa

U. S. citizens with Iowa residence entering the University of Northern Iowa may apply for aid of $530 renewable for four years.

Write to
Director of Financial Aid
University of Northern Iowa
Cedar Falls, IA 50613

State of Iowa Scholarship Program

Funds from $100 to $600 assist high school graduates who are U. S. citizens and Iowa residents planning to attend an approved Iowa college or university, Area Community School or school of professional nursing.

Applicants should take American College Test (ACT) on any test date between October of junior year and October of senior year of high school. Students identified as State of Iowa Scholars on the basis of ACT scores and class rank will be invited to compete for award by filing a Parents' Confidential Statement with the College Scholarship Service by January 18 of year prior to award.

Write to
State of Iowa Scholarship Program
Higher Education Facilities Commission
201 Jewett Building
Ninth and Grand
Des Moines, IA 50309

University of Iowa

Students entering the University of Iowa should apply for freshman scholarships. Awards based on need and academic record. Must be in upper 10 percent of class or have an ACT score (composite) of 28 or higher. Amounts determined by university.

Write to
Director of Financial Aid
University of Iowa
Iowa City, IA 52240

Rehabilitation Services

Tuition, fees and other assistance offered to disabled students at Iowa State University, University of Iowa, University of Northern Iowa and other training facilities.

Write to
Branch Rehabilitation Education & Services
801 Bankers Trust Building
Des Moines, IA 50309

Higher Education Facilities Commission
Grants from the commission vary from $50 to $1,000, depending on need, but may not exceed tuition and fees minus the average amount the student would pay at a state university. Students enrolled at Iowa private colleges are eligible and must file a Parents' Confidential Statement. Apply no later than January 1 prior to award.

Write to
Higher Education Facilities Commission
201 Jewett Building
Ninth and Grand
Des Moines, IA 50309

For information about guaranteed loans, write to:
Director of Higher Education, Office of Education, Region VII,
601 E. 12th Street, Kansas City, MO 64106

Kansas

Tuition Grant Program
A maximum of $1,000 is offered to Kansas students to attend a fully accredited Kansas independent college. Monies are to be applied to tuition and required fees.

Write to
Tuition Grant Program
State Education Commission
700 Kansas Avenue
Topeka, KS 66612

State Scholarships Programs
Resident Kansas students may apply for $500 freshmen awards which are renewable for sophomore year. These are for use at any accredited Kansas college or university.

Write to
State Scholarship Programs
State Department of Education
120 E. 10th Street
Topeka, KS 66612

For information about guaranteed loans, write to:
Director of Higher Education, Office of Education, Region VII,
601 E. 12th Street, Kansas City, MO 64106

Kentucky

Bureau of Rehabilitation
Resident students who are disabled and can demonstrate financial need, academic aptitude, good citizenship and character are eligible for a partial to full payment of tuition, books and other fees with renewable privileges.

Write to
Bureau of Rehabilitation
State Department of Education
State Office Building
Frankfort, KY 40601

Higher Education Assistance Authority
Based on need and the availability of funds, grants are made to resident students accepted as full-time students in an approved Kentucky non-profit college or university who are not enrolled in a course of study leading to a degree in theology, divinity or religious education, and who have no more than seven semesters (or the equivalent) of completed education.

Write to
Kentucky Higher Education Assistance Authority
319 Ann Street
Frankfort, KY 40601

Kentucky Dental Association
College graduates of five years residence are eligible for $1,500 (per year for four years) when accepted for enrollment in an accredited dental school. Must agree to practice one year in an assigned locality for each $1,500 received.

Write to
Kentucky Dental Association
1940 Princeton Drive
Louisville, KY 40205

Honor scholarships based on need are available for Kentucky residents. Information is offered through the college of student's choice.

Kentucky Medical Association

Residents of Kentucky who have been admitted to an accredited medical school may request loans of up to $2,500 per year. Recipients must agree to practice in rural Kentucky for one year for each loan received. Persons may also practice with the Kentucky Public Health Service in an approved area.

Write to
Rural Kentucky Medical Scholarship Fund
Kentucky Medical Association
3532 Ephraim McDowell Drive
Louisville, KY 40205

For information about guaranteed loans, write to:
Director of Higher Education, Office of Education, Region IV,
50 Seventh Street NE, Atlanta, GA 30323

Louisiana

State Superintendent of Education

Academic scholarships of $600 are awarded on the basis of achievement, testing, interviews and recommendations of high school teachers and principals.

Write to
State Superintendent of Education
Baton Rouge, LA 70804

T. H. Harris Scholarships

Write to above address for information on these funds for use at state-supported colleges and universities except Airline, Delgado and St. Bernard. Number and amount of scholarship varies. Maximum is $300.

Louisiana Stonewall Jackson Memorial Board Scholarship

Write to State Superintendent of Education (listed above) for information on grants to high school students entering essay competitions. Students must attend a Louisiana institution of higher learning.

Fee Exemptions

The State Superintendent of Education offers fee exemption scholarships for the following: Board of Supervisors, band and

207

orchestra, ministerial, 4H Club, Future Farmers of America and Pelican State.

Through high school principals scholarships are available (amount to be determined by the State Board of Education) awarded annually to a graduate in the upper one-third of each graduating class of twenty-five or less. More scholarships are available in larger schools.

Outstanding freshman students are considered for renewable Louisiana State University Centennial Honor Awards of $100 to $750 per year. Information is obtained from Committee of Student Employment and Scholarships at college where student is admitted as a freshman.

Department of Hospitals
This aid is for students desiring further education for improved training as special educators, nurse anesthetists, occupational therapists, medical students, interns, resident physicians, medical records librarians, medical technologists, physical therapists, speech therapists, X-ray technicians and other professional trainees for the purposes of enhancing their employment possibilities with state owned and operated hospitals, and in schools and day-care centers for the mentally retarded.

Write to
Training Officer
Department of Hospitals
655 No. 5th Street
Baton Rouge, LA 70804

Nursing Training Programs
The Department of Hospitals assists students with stipends (of varying amounts) to complete nursing training if the students agree to be employed at one of the state hospitals for time equivalent to that for which the stipend was received.

Write to Department of Hospitals at the address listed above.

Details of $100 per month in the Diploma Nurse Training programs are available from the admission officer of school selected within the state.

For information about guaranteed loans, write to:

208

*(In-State Students) Louisiana Higher Education Assistance Commission,
P.O. Box 44095, Capitol Station, Baton Rouge, LA 70802;
(Out-of-State Students) United Student Aid Funds, Inc.,
5259 N. Tacoma Avenue, Indianapolis, IN 46220*

Maine

University of Maine
Awards in values up to full tuition are available to students in attendance at the University of Maine.

Write to
Student Aid Office
University of Maine
Orono, ME 04473

Write to student aid offices at the college of student's choice for further facts on the following:
Students accepted or enrolled at any of the campuses of the University of Maine system are eligible for awards in varying amounts according to need. Parents' Confidential Statement is required.

Room, board, tuition and required fees for North American Indians, (one-year residents of Maine) who are included on a tribal census, or whose parents or grandparents were so included, and who have been accepted at one of the campuses of the University of Maine system.

*For information about guaranteed loans, write to:
United Student Aid Funds, Inc.,
5259 North Tacoma Avenue, Indianapolis, IN 46220*

Maryland

State Scholarship Board
General State Scholarships are for resident high school seniors or previous graduates accepted as full-time students. Awards of $200 to $1,500 are offered at Maryland degree-granting institutions including junior and community colleges.

Write to
State Scholarship Board
Baltimore, MD 21218

Write to the above address for details on assistance (reimbursement of tuition upon completion of course of study) to regular paid and

209

volunteer firemen engaged in the profession in the state for study programs in fire service technology.

The State Scholarship Board also offers facts on state senators' nominations from respective districts. Selection for the $250 to $1,500 scholarships is made from a competitive examination listing.

Likewise, each member of the House of Delegates may appoint two students from the respective district for free tuition at the University of Maryland, College Park. Appointees are selected on no special basis. Contact the State Scholarship Board through the address listed above.

Ten medical scholarships of $1,500 per year are awarded annually to students who have been residents of Maryland at least five years and have received the bachelor's degree from an accredited college. Recipients agree to practice three years in an area of medical need in Maryland. Apply before April 1 to State Scholarship Board address given above.

University of Maryland
Twelve fellowships ($2,500 maximum for three years) are awarded to graduates of an accredited four-year college for post-graduate work in the graduate school of the University of Maryland at College Park. Recipients agree to teach in a public institution of higher learning in Maryland.

Write to
University of Maryland
Fellowship Office, Graduate School
College Park, MD 20470

Professional School Scholarships
Money ($200 to $1,000, based on need) is available for students who are three-year residents of Maryland prior to award for use in professional schools of medicine, dentistry, law, nursing and pharmacy. Details and application obtainable through financial aid director of school selected by student.

State Scholarship Board
Recommended senior undergraduates or candidates for a master's degree in education of the deaf may receive aid equal to tuition at the selected training center. Awards are based on financial need.

Write to
State Scholarship Board
2100 Guilford Avenue
Baltimore, MD 21218

Fireman Association

Persons sixteen to twenty-three with a parent killed in line of duty as a volunteer fireman in Maryland are eligible for a maximum of $500 to be applied toward tuition, matriculation fees, room, board, books and supplies.

Write to
Fireman Association
Route 1, Box 523
Frostberg, MD 21532

For information about guaranteed loans, write to:
Maryland Higher Education Loan Corporation
2100 Guilford Avenue
Baltimore, MD 21218

Massachusetts

Department of Education

Four Commonwealth scholarships (free tuition for four years at the University of Massachusetts, a state college or state technologial institute) in each senatorial district are awarded to resident students who achieve the four highest marks in a competitive examination.

Write to
Department of Education
Commonwealth of Massachusetts
182 Tremont Street
Boston, MA 02111

The department can also be contacted for details on the following programs:

Partial or full scholarships for needy and worthy students with minimum residence of four consecutive years prior to application can be applied to study in medical and dental schools and recognized schools of nursing.

Scholarships exist for Massachusetts high school graduates whose parent is a deceased member of paid fire or police departments where injuries were received in the performance of duty. Funds cover tuition at an institution operated by the Commonwealth. Aid applies also to Metropolitan District Commission or the Capitol Police.

Special education scholarships are offered to undergraduates who plan to become certified teachers of the mentally retarded. Applicants must be needy and academically worthy full-time students domiciled in Massachusetts in order to qualify for funds (not to exceed $500 per year for three years).

Needy and worthy full-time undergraduates (Commonwealth residents) may apply for $200 in public-supported institutions and $700 in private institutions at any regionally-accredited institution in the U.S. In Massachusetts, awards must be used at institutions approved for degree authority by the Board of Higher Education.

For information on guaranteed loans, write to:
Massachusetts Higher Education Assistance Corporation
511 Statler Building, Boston, MA 02116

Fitchburg State College
Special education scholarships—upon recommendation of the college president—are obtainable for high school graduates of the Commonwealth who enter the State College at Fitchburg for training as teachers of the mentally retarded. Awards are for $300 for not more than four years.

Write to
President
State College
Fitchburg, MA 01420

University of Massachusetts, Amherst
University of Massachusetts, Boston
Scholarships (amounts determined by state appropriation) and grants are available for members of each of the four undergraduate classes who have a financial need and who have attained the scholarship requirements of the University Committee on Financial Aid.

Write to
Director of Financial Aid
University of Massachusetts
Amherst, MA 01002

or

Director of Financial Aid
University of Massachusetts
Boston, MA 02116

212

Michigan

Department of Education

A Michigan Competitive Scholarship or Tuition Grant is awarded to students of good moral character who have been residents of Michigan for eighteen months, who are high school graduates, and who plan to attend college full-time. Scholarship applicants may attend any approved college or university in Michigan. (Limited to tuition and fees.) Tuition grant applicants may attend an eligible private, non-profit college or university in Michigan.

Write to

Department of Education
Division of Student Financial Aids
P. O. Box 420
Lansing, MI 48902

For information about guaranteed loans, write to:
Michigan Higher Education Assistance Authority,
700 Prudential Building, Box 420, Lansing, MI 48902

Minnesota

Minnesota Board of Nursing

Resident students of ability and financial need accepted by approved schools preparing students for registered or practical nursing are eligible for funds ($2,000 maximum for registered nurse programs and $300 for practical nurse programs). Recipients must practice one year in Minnesota following graduation.

Write to

Minnesota Board of Nursing
393 No. Dunlap Street
St. Paul, MN 55104

Minnesota Higher Education Coordinating Commission

Renewable state scholarships determined by financial need are extended to Minnesota residents ranked in upper quartile of high school class. Recipient must enter a Minnesota approved college, university or vocational school.

Write to

Minnesota Higher Education Coordinating Commission
Suite 400, Capitol Square
550 Cedar Street
St. Paul, MN 55101

213

Contact the above address for details about the State Grant-in-Aid extended to Minnesota residents, regardless of class rank. Applicants for the maximum of $1,000 annually must be needy and must plan to enter a Minnesota approved college, university or vocational school.

State Department of Public Welfare

Assistance is available for graduate training in social work. The maximum award for a single person is $2,250; married, $2,700; married plus one child, $3,150; married plus two or more children, $3,600. Additional allowances up to $1,200 per school year for tuition expenses is attached. Eligibility is determined only by admission to an approved graduate school of social work in the U. S. or Canada.

Write to

Personnel Director
State Department of Public Welfare
Centennial Building
St. Paul, MN 55101

Write to the same address for information on aid for advanced training in psychiatric nursing. Applicants for amounts specified above for social work must be registered nurses and must be accepted at an approved school of psychiatric nursing.

The State Department of Public Welfare also offers grants of comparable amounts to juniors and seniors who have been accepted at schools offering approved courses leading toward certification in occupational therapy.

Acceptance in a graduate school offering approved courses leading to a master's degree in hospital recreation or recreational therapy is the only eligibility requirement for State Department of Public Welfare funds covering tuition and stipend. Write to the address listed.

Baccalaureate, diploma and licensed practical nursing programs also come under the State Department of Public Welfare. Contact the department for information on these programs at schools approved by the Minnesota Board of Nursing. Monthly award for a single person is $250; married, $300; married, one child, $350; married, two or more children, $400.

For information about guaranteed loans, write to:
Director of Higher Education, Office of Education, Region V,
226 W. Jackson Boulevard, Chicago, IL 60606

Mississippi

Professional and Graduate Education Program

Scholarship aid is extended for pursuit of graduate or professional work in out-of-state institutions. Applicant must have been a legal resident of Mississippi for one year prior to date of application and must qualify for graduate or professional courses not available in regularly supported Mississippi institutions of higher education.

Write to
Professional and Graduate Education Program
P. O. Box 2336
Jackson, MS 39205

Board of Trustees

College Scholarships are available for children of law officers and full-time firemen fatally injured or totally disabled from injuries which occurred in the performance of their official duties.

Write to
Board of Trustees
Institutions of Higher Learning
P. O. Box 2336
Jackson, MS 39205

For information about guaranteed loans, write to:
Director of Higher Education, Office of Education, Region IV,
50 Seventh Street NE, Atlanta, GA 30323

Missouri

Residents of Missouri who score high on the Ohio Psychological Test (administered on a statewide basis) are eligible for scholarships to apply toward tuition and incidental fees. Those interested should apply through the registrars of state colleges at Warrensburg, Maryville, Kirksville, Cape Girardeau or Springfield, or the University of Missouri.

For information about guaranteed loans, write to:
United Student Aid Funds, Inc.,
5259 N. Tacoma Avenue, Indianapolis, IN 46220

Montana

Apply through the institution of the student's choice for the following aid:

Advanced Honor Scholarship

A waiver of fees (approximately $225 per year) is awarded to a qualified student at the conclusion of the freshman year of college.

215

Non-resident fee may be waived in the case of an out-of-state student. Waiver based on scholarship, promise and character.

Fee waivers are granted to Indians (Montana residents) of at least one-fourth Indian ancestry.

Information is available through the high school principal for High School Honor Scholarships. Grant waives fees for freshman year only.

For information about guaranteed loans, write to:
Director of Higher Education, Office of Education, Region VIII,
9017 Federal Office Building, 19th and Stout Streets, Denver, CO 80202

Nebraska

High school principals or counselors have information on approximately three hundred Regents Scholarships awarded annually at the University of Nebraska to resident students in the upper one-fourth of their graduating class. Based on competitive examination.

Department of Agriculture

Nebraska farm or ranch youths who need financial assistance to pursue education beyond high school may receive low interest loans up to $1,500 per year. Recipients must enroll in an institution owned or controlled by the state or a government subdivision thereof.

Write to
Department of Agriculture
P. O. Box 4844
State Capitol
Lincoln, NB 68509

For information about guaranteed loans, write to:
Director of Higher Education, Office of Education, Region VII,
601 E. 12th Street, Kansas City, MO 64108

Nevada

Resident students are not charged tuition at state-supported universities. After six months' residence in Nevada, military personnel are eligible for resident fees. Children of military personnel are not charged non-resident fees if the parent has lived in the state six months. For further details, write to the director of admissions at college selected.

For information about guaranteed loans, write to:
United Student Aid Funds, Inc.,
5259 N. Tacoma Avenue, Indianapolis, IN 46220

New Hampshire

Keene State College
Plymouth State College
Student of state colleges with teaching majors, good scholastic standing, leadership ability and financial need who agree to teach in New Hampshire one year for every year assisted are eligible for aid of $200 a year maximum (renewable).

Write to
Director of Student Personnel
Keene State College
Keene, NH 03431

or

Director of Student Personnel
Plymouth State College
Plymouth, NH 03264

Board of Nursing Education
Qualifications for up to $1,200 for three years (of which not more than $400 may be awarded for any one year) include financial need and New Hampshire residence. In addition, applicant must be accepted in a New Hampshire approved school of nursing and must agree to practice in the state for one year following graduation and licensure.

Write to
New Hampshire State Board of Nursing
Education and Nurse Registration
105 Loudon Road
Concord, NH 03301

For information about guaranteed loans, write to:
New Hampshire Higher Education Assistance Foundation,
3 Capitol Street, Concord, NH 03301

New Jersey

Department of Higher Education
Satisfactory scholarship record, financial need, demonstrated moral character, good citizenship, and dedication to American ideals qualify New Jersey residents for State Competitive Scholarships. Applicants for the $500 a year grants (or amount charged for tuition, whichever is smaller) must have graduated, or will graduate, within one year of application.

Write to

217

Department of Higher Education
Office of Student Financial Aid
225 W. State Street
Trenton, NJ 08625

Apply to the above address for Incentive Scholarships. Basic awards to meet the cost of tuition and fees in amounts of $100 to $500 are slated for students attending New Jersey schools. For further eligibility requirements, apply to the Department of Higher Education.

New Jersey residents with demonstrated need, and who are graduates of New Jersey county colleges, with plans to attend four-year institutions full-time, are eligible for $500 (or tuition, whichever is less. Renewable). Write to Department of Higher Education at address listed above.

Tuition aid grants of $200 to $1,000 are earmarked for New Jersey residents enrolled at a New Jersey college or university. Aid granted on the basis of need where tuition exceeds $450. Apply to Department of Higher Education at address listed above.

For information about guaranteed loans, write to:
New Jersey Higher Education Assistance Authority,
225 W. State Street, Trenton, NJ 08625

New Mexico

New Mexico universities and colleges have discretionary power to award and grant scholarships (matriculation fees or tuition, or both) to students who have state residence, high moral character and scholastic standing. Contact state colleges and universities.

For information about guaranteed loans, write to:
Director of Higher Education, Office of Education, Region VI,
1114 Commerce Street, Dallas, TX 75202

New York

Regents Examination and Scholarship Center
Resident students of New York seeking full-time study in approved schools of nursing in the state are eligible for $200 to $500 depending on need (four years maximum).

Write to
Regents Examination and Scholarship Center
State Education Department
Albany, NY 12224

Write to the above address for details on $100 to $1,000 (depending on need; four or five years maximum) offered to resident students who will attend Cornell University (including the New York State Colleges at Cornell University).

Scholar incentive awards ($100 to $600 yearly) are available for legal residents enrolled in a full-time program of study leading to a degree at a college or hospital school of nursing, trade or technical school, or in a two-year program in a registered private business school in the state which has tuition in excess of $200.

Accredited schools grant scholarships to children of state and local corrections officers, civilian employees of a correctional facility, as well as law enforcement personnel throughout the state who died in the line of duty. Must attend accredited school of higher education in New York State and must apply through respective financial aid offices.

Regents Examination and Scholarship Center
New York residents studying medicine or dentistry in an approved medical or dental school in New York State, or in an approved school of osteopathy in the United States, may receive up to $1,000 per year depending on need.

Write to
Regents Examination and Scholarship Center
State Education Department
Albany, NY 12224

State University of New York
State University Scholarships are awarded to students who are legal residents and who have enormous learning deficiency because of color, income level, family and/or neighborhood background. Intent of the program is to fill the gap between the formal high school curriculum and the entering level at a two- or four-year college program. Funds are available at state university campuses including thirty-three community colleges.

Write to
State University of New York
8 Thurlow Terrace
Albany, NY 12201

For information about guaranteed loans, write to:
New York Higher Education Assistance Corporation
50 Wolf Road, Albany, NY 12205

North Carolina

Medical Care Commission

Students of one-year residence immediately preceding full-time enrollment in dentistry, medicine, pharmacy, nursing, nurse anesthesia, medical technology, optometry, physical therapy, medical records library science, occupational therapy, dietetics, medical social work, clinical psychology, medical sociology, sociology of health, osteopathy, medical recreation or public health (physicians only) may receive grants from commission. (Contact the commission for amounts.) Students must agree to practice in North Carolina a full calendar year or fraction thereof for which a loan is received. Otherwise, payment is due upon demand at 7 percent interest per year.

Write to

The North Carolina Medical Care Commission
P. O. Box 25459
437 No. Harrington Street
Raleigh, NC 27611

Prospective Teachers Scholarship Loan Fund

Resident students interested in a career in teaching may receive $600 annually (renewable).

Write to

Prospective Teachers Scholarship Loan Fund
State Department of Public Instruction
Raleigh, NC 27602

For those currently teaching in North Carolina with less than an A certificate, summer school scholarships of $75 each are available. Write to above address.

Scholarships for Teachers of the Mentally Retarded

Renewable scholarships of $900 are extended to full-time enrollees planning to teach the mentally retarded.

Write to

Scholarships for Teachers of the Mentally Retarded
State Department of Public Instruction
Raleigh, NC 27602

For information about guaranteed loans, write to:
State Education Assistance Authority, 1307 Glenwood Avenue,
Raleigh, NC 27605

North Dakota

Nursing Scholarship Loan Committee

Residents of North Dakota who agree to practice in the state one year or repay amount of loan plus interest are eligible for $300 (for practical nursing programs).

Write to

North Dakota Nursing Scholarship Loan Committee
219 No. 7th Street
Bismarck, ND 58501

Residents of North Dakota who agree to practice two years in the state or repay amount of loan plus interest are eligible for $1,000 (for two-year, three-year or four-year nursing programs). Write to above address.

Acceptance of two years of employment entitles North Dakota residents to $1,800 for a graduate nursing program. Write to above address.

University of North Dakota

Medical students in third year and fourth year of schooling are eligible for a maximum grant of $2,500 per year. Five years of practice in a small town in North Dakota cancels debt.

Write to

Dean, School of Medicine
University of North Dakota
Grand Forks, ND 58201

State Highway Department

A student who has completed one year of college in civil engineering or in civil engineering technology, and who agrees to accept employment or repayment of loan, may receive $600 per year for three years at either the University of North Dakota or North Dakota State University.

Write to

Commissioner,
North Dakota State Highway Department
Bismarck, ND 58501

Resident students who demonstrate academic aptitude, need, good citizenship and good character may receive funds for school fees. Apply to North Dakota state institution of choice.

For information about guaranteed loans, write to:
Director of Higher Education, Office of Education, Region VIII,
Federal Office Building, Room 9017, 19th and Stout Streets,
Denver, CO 90202

Ohio

The Ohio Instructional Grants Program is aid extended to assist resident students having exceptional financial need as undergraduates in an eligible Ohio institution of higher education. Information can be obtained from high schools or from the college or university the student wishes to attend.

For information about guaranteed loans, write to:
Ohio Student Loan Association, Wyandotte Building,
21 W. Broad Street, Columbus, OH 43215

Oklahoma

Schools of the Oklahoma state system are authorized to waive enrollment fees as a scholarship benefit. Interested students should contact the high school counselor or the admissions officer of respective colleges.

For information about guaranteed loans, write to:
Oklahoma State Regents for Higher Education, State Capitol,
State Capitol Station, Box 533893, Oklahoma City. OK 73105

Oregon

Contact the high school principal or counselor for information on the folowing aid opportunities:

Four-year state cash awards are available to Oregon residents at two-year and four-year public and private accredited degree-granting institutions in Oregon. Renewal is dependent on student's academic standing and continued financial need.

Community College Awards of $300 or the amount of tuition and all fees (whichever is less) are available (on the basis of financial need) to Oregon residents at two-year community colleges located in Oregon.

Need Grant Programs (not to exceed 50 percent of student's computed financial need) are extended to Oregon residents at any two-year or four-year, non-profit, generally accredited institution in the state. Also, grants are applicable at any hospital school of nursing located in Oregon and accredited by the National League of Nursing. Applicant

222

must meet institution's entrance requirements and must demonstrate financial need.

For information about guaranteed loans, write to:
State of Oregon Scholarship Commission, Box 3175, Eugene, OR 97401

Pennsylvania

Each state senator may award partial tuition scholarships to students entering state schools. Awards are renewable where grades meet standards above minimum passing requirements. Students must be resident and must attend full-time. Requests should be addressed to state senators.

Higher Education Assistance Agency
Depending on appropriation of funds, needy secondary school graduates may receive aid to attend the college of their choice. Applicants must be enrolled full-time in an approved institution, must be of satisfactory character, must be a U. S. citizen or must be taking steps to become a citizen, and must have been a state resident for at least one year prior to application. Applications may be made by current high school graduates, upper-classmen attending approved institutions, and students who have had a year or more lapse between secondary school graduation and college enrollment.

Write to
Pennsylvania Higher Education Assistance Agency
Towne House
Harrisburg, PA 17102

For information about guaranteed loans, write to:
Pennsylvania Higher Education Assistance Agency, Towne House,
660 Boas Street, Harrisburg, PA 17102

Puerto Rico

For information about guaranteed loans, write to:
Director of Higher Education, Office of Education, Region IV,
50 Seventh Street NE, Atlanta, GA 30323

Rhode Island

Deputy Commissioner of Education
Rhode Island State Scholarships are available to 5 percent of graduating classes of public and private secondary schools based on

scholastic records and financial need.

Write to
Deputy Commissioner of Education
State Department of Education
Roger Williams Building
Hayes Street
Providence, RI 02908

Undergraduate study in nursing education is subsidized for qualified high school graduates. Make application through college, hospital or State Department of Education at address listed above.

Deputy Commissioner of Education
The Deputy Commissioner offers aid of varying amounts to those seeking post graduate study in registered nursing.

Write to
Deputy Commissioner of Education
State Department of Education
Roger Williams Building
Hayes Street
Providence, RI 02908

Division of Vocational Rehabilitation
Anyone physically or emotionally handicapped may be assisted (with aid determined by the division) through academic, vocational or on-the-job training in attaining a vocational objective within his or her physical and mental capacity.

Write to
Division of Vocational Rehabilitation
Fountain Street
Providence, RI 02919

Bryant College
Two years' residence and agreement to teach business in Rhode Island for two years after completion of study qualifies students for full tuition awards. Make application before February 1.

Write to
Registrar
Bryant College
Smithfield, RI 02917

For information about guaranteed loans, write to:
Rhode Island Higher Education Assistance Corporation
139 Mathewson Street, Room 404, Providence, RI 02901

South Carolina

Students may apply to the financial aid director of the college of their choice for details of available scholarships and grants.

American Legion
Veterans should apply to the American Legion for full information on veterans benefits.

Write to
Department Headquarters
American Legion
132 Pickens Street
P. O. Box 11355
Columbia, SC 29205

For information about guaranteed loans, write to:
United Student Aid Funds, Inc.,
5259 N. Tacoma Avenue, Indianapolis, IN 46220

South Dakota

Contact the college of student's choice for details on the following:

Resident students who served honorably in the armed forces in any war (including Red Cross service) may receive full tuition (unless federal educational aid is being given) for use at a state institution under control and management of the South Dakota Board of Regents.

Blind students attending state educational institutions may receive full tuition and fee scholarships. (Degree of sight loss must be established by an opthalmologist recognized by Social Service Board.)

For information about guaranteed loans, write to:
Director of Higher Education, Office of Education, Region VIII,
Room 9017, Federal Office Building, 19th and Stout Streets
Denver, CO 80202

Tennessee

Contact chairman of scholarship committee at state college or university selected by the student for information on academic scholarships (amount to be determined by school) for high school graduates attending state colleges and universities.

For information on guaranteed loans, write to:
Tennessee Education Loan Corporation, State Department of Education,
313 Capitol Towers, Nashville, TN 37219

Texas

The high school guidance counselor or financial aid·officer of selected institution has facts and applications for the following Texas programs:

Exemption from payment of tuition and fees for blind students.

Payment of tuition and fees for high school graduates boarded at state orphanages.

Tuition fees for two semesters paid for the highest-ranking graduate of accredited high schools.

Payment of tuition fees (one year) for certain students from other nations in the Americas.

Resident student tuition fees offered to members of the armed forces stationed in Texas.

Resident tuition fees extended to teachers, professors and/or other employees of the state institutions of higher learning, their husbands or wives (as the case may be) and their children.

The Connally-Carrillo Act exempting tuition fees for persons with family incomes of not more than $4,800.

Exemption of tuition and fees for dependent children of Texas military personnel listed as missing in action or as prisoners-of-war.

Exemption of certain students from payment of part of tuition where hardship was created as a result of tuition increases passed by the 1957 legislature.

Payment of tuition and lab fees amounting to approximately $110 for a nine-month session waived for children of certain firemen, peace officers, employees of Texas Department of Corrections and game wardens.

Scholarships determined by institution (extended to needy resident and non-resident students), and based on financial need, character and scholastic record.

Provision, by the Coordinating Board, Texas College and University System, or equalization grants to Texas residents enrolled as full-time students in approved private Texas colleges or universities. (Awarded on a financial-need basis.)

For information about Direct State loans, write to:

226

Director of Student Financial Aid, Texas College and University System, Sam Houston State Office Building, 201 E 14th Street, Austin TX 78701; guaranteed loans, write to: Director of Higher Education, Office of Education, Region VI, 1114 Commerce Street, Dallas, TX, 75202

Utah

Scholarships Award Committee
Resident students at the University of Utah are granted tuition funds based on grades, talent, leadership and need.

Write to
Scholarships Award Committee
University of Utah
Salt Lake City, UT 84100

For information about guaranteed loans, write to:
Director of Higher Education, Office of Education Region VIII, Federal Office Building, Room 9017, 19th and Stout Streets, Denver, CO 80202

Vermont

Resident students attending Bennington, Castleton State, Goddard, Johnson State, Lyndon State, Marlboro, Middlebury, Trinity, St. Michael's or Windham Colleges, or a Vermont school of nursing, the University of Vermont or Norwich University, may contact the county senator or director of admissions at appropriate schools for details on partial tuition payments (renewable).

For information about guaranteed loans, write to:
Vermont Student Assistance Corporation
109 S. Winowski Avenue,
Burlington, VT 05401

Virginia

Virginia Commonwealth University
Resident dental students at Virginia Commonwealth University School of Dentistry who agree to practice with the State Health Department for one year for each year assisted are eligible for annual awards of $1,500.

Write to
Dean, School of Dentistry
Virginia Commonwealth University
Richmond, VA 23219

Division of Dental Health

Dental hygienists at Virginia Commonwealth University or at Old Dominion University who agree to practice dental hygiene in Virginia for each year assisted may receive an annual award of $500.

Write to
Division of Dental Health
109 Governor Street
Richmond, VA 23219

State Health Department

Resident student nurses attending an approved Virginia school of nursing who agree to practice for a period of time related to amount and number of scholarships received are eligible for $250 to $1,000.

Write to
State Health Department
Director, Bureau of Public Nursing
109 Governor Street
Richmond, VA 23219

Write to the same address for details on assistance ($500 to $2,000 annually) for registered professional nurses (those seeking B.S. or higher degrees) who agree to practice in Virginia in positions related to type of preparation for period of time determined by amount and number of scholarships.

Virginia Commonwealth University

Resident medical students at Virginia Commonwealth University Medical College who agree to engage continuously in the practice of family medicine in an area of need in Virginia for a period of time equal to number of years assisted, or as determined by the State Health Commissioner, are offered $2,500 annually.

Write to
Associate Dean, School of Medicine
Virginia Commonwealth University
Richmond, VA 23219

For information about guaranteed loans, write to:
(In-State students) Virginia State Education Assistance Authority,
1116 United Virginia Bank Building, Richmond, VA 23216;
(Out-of-State students) Director of Higher Education,
Office of Education, Region III, 401 N. Broad Street,
Philadelphia, PA 19108

Virgin Islands

For information about guaranteed loans, write to:
United Student Aid Funds, Inc.,
5259 N. Tacoma Avenue, Indianapolis, IN 46220

Washington

State Board of Education
Legally blind students admitted to an institution of higher education, and who are in need of assistance, are eligible for tuition and lab fee aid not to exceed $200 per quarter.

Write to
State Board of Education
Olympia, WA 98504

For information about guaranteed loans, write to:
Director of Higher Education, Office of Education, Region X,
1319 2nd Avenue, Seattle, WA 98101

West Virginia

Commission of Higher Education
Applicants for $100 to $900 must be high school graduates or must have the equivalent of a high school diploma and must demonstrate need for financial assistance to attend the college of his or her choice. Applicant must be enrolled full-time at a college or university in the state, must be a citizen of the United States, must be a resident of West Virginia prior to application, must meet the admissions requirements of the selected institution and must be an undergraduate student of good moral character.

Write to
West Virginia Commission of Higher Education
1316 Charleston National Plaza
Charleston, WV 25301

For information about guaranteed loans, write to:
Director of Higher Education, Office of Education, Region III,
401 N. Broad Street, Philadelphia, PA 19108

Wisconsin

Tuition Grant Program
Undergraduate tuition grants are available to residents in good academic standing at Wisconsin private institutions. Awards (based on

229

difference between public and private tuition charges) are granted according to need.

Write to
Wisconsin Tuition Grant Program
Higher Educational Aids Board
115 West Wilson Street
Madison, WI 53703

Wisconsin Honor Scholarship Program
Honor scholarships are available to graduating high school seniors. Awards are based on academic achievement in high school as shown by rank in the top 10 percent of the graduating class. Students must be Wisconsin residents and must attend a Wisconsin public or private institution. The program (providing up to $800) is for freshman year only.

Write to
Wisconsin Honor Scholarship Program
Higher Educational Aids Boards
115 West Wilson Street
Madison, WI 53703

Address inquiries about Tuition Reimbursement Program to the above address. Grants of up to $500 per year are open to residents enrolled at private institutions in Wisconsin and at public or private institutions outside Wisconsin in courses leading to a first professional degree in programs not offered in Wisconsin public institutions.

Non-resident members of the armed forces (and their dependents) stationed in the state should contact the registrar at school of student's choice for facts on exemption from tuition and fees.

The State Board of Nursing may grant scholarships to qualified nurses who desire to become nursing school instructors or administrative personnel in accredited schools of professional and practical nursing in Wisconsin. Apply to Wisconsin State Board of Nursing.

Division of Family Services (or whichever of the following is applicable): **Division of Mental Hygiene, Division of Corrections, Division of Vocational Rehabilitation)**

The State Department of Health and Social Services (through the above named divisions) grants stipends to qualified applicants who desire to become graduate social workers or rehabilitative counselors in public

230

agencies in Wisconsin. Applicants must have a B. A. degree and must meet entrance requirements of accredited graduate schools. Address inquiry to the appropriate division.

Write to
State Department of Health and Social Services
1 West Wilson Street
Madison, WI 53702

For information about guaranteed loans, write to:
Wisconsin Higher Education Corporation, State Office Building,
115 W. Wilson Street, Madison, WI 53702

Wyoming

Students selected on the basis of need, character, extra-curricular activities and scholastic ability are eligible for County Commissioner Scholarships of $150.75 per semester. Contact commissioner in county of residence.

Wyoming high school honor student scholarships in the amount of $111 (for eight semesters) are available for use at the University of Wyoming. High school principal should be contacted for details.

For information about guaranteed loans, write to:
Director, Higher Education, Office of Education, Region VIII,
Federal Office Building, Room 9017,
19th and Stout Streets, Denver, CO 80202

Private and Limited Eligibility Funds

Many students with interest in a professional area are eligible for aid established to promote entrance into that field. Industry and private organizations often make a commitment to higher education by offering scholarships and loans to worthy students, while some agencies act as consultants which students may write or call for information about sources often overlooked. We can provide information about only a few of the numerous financial aid sources. It is hoped that the student will be motivated to seek additional information from his or her high school counselor and/or principal and from the admissions officers of the colleges selected. The public library is also an excellent repository for such information. Below are listed several more sources of financial aid. Some are listed according to profession. Eligibility requirements are given in cases where information was

231

available. For additional information see the section on *Financial Aid Restricted to Health-Related Careers,* p. 248 and, *to Minorities,* p. 250 and to *Regions* p. 258.

Consultant Agency

National Scholarship Service and Fund for Negro Students

The Fund is primarily a college advisory and referral service (provided at no charge) for black high school students. Funds disbursed through NSSFNS are sometimes restricted by the contributor to certain major fields of study, sex, or geographical location, and are available only to students counseled by NSSFNS.

Write to
National Scholarship Service and Fund for Negro Students
1776 Broadway
New York, NY 10019

Architecture and Engineering

The American Institute of Architects

The Institute offers one scholarship (amount determined by the institute) to a student interested in architecture as a career.

Write to
American Institute of Architects
110 Pearl Street
Buffalo, NY 14202

The Cooper Union for the Advancement of Science and Art

Scholarships valued at $1,500 to $2,000 are awarded on the basis of standing in competition. Funds offered in art, architecture, engineering and science.

Write to
The Cooper Union
New York, NY 10003

Antioch-Niagara Frontier Council

Two scholarships, from $400 to $800, are offered for studies in engineering.

232

Write to
Antioch-Niagara Frontier Council
116 Hartwell Road
Buffalo, NY 14216

Polytechnic Institute of Brooklyn
Students wishing to graduate in electrical engineering are eligible.
Special consideration given those from black high schools in the South.
Grant includes tuition and all maintenance costs.

Write to
Director
Polytechnic Institute of Brooklyn
Brooklyn, NY 11201

Union Carbide Education Fund
The fund extends awards of varying amounts administered through
thirty-five engineering colleges and universities.

Write to
Union Carbide Education Fund
270 Park Avenue
New York, NY 10017

Lockheed Leadership Fund
The Lockheed Company offers ten awards in engineering and five in
other fields. Scholarships cover tuition fees and have a $500 stipend.
Write to admissions director of selected college.

American Institute of Steel Construction, Inc.
Non-renewable awards of $3,000 are awarded to senior graduate civil
or architectural engineering students.

Write to
American Institute of Steel Construction, Inc.
101 Park Avenue
New York, NY 10017

Allegheny-Ludlum Industries, Inc.
While some of the company's scholarships are limited to sons and
daughters of employees, A-L also makes awards to engineering
students entering their sophomore year ($700; renewable).

Write to
Allegheny-Ludlum Industries, Inc.
2000 Oliver Building
Pittsburgh, PA 15222

The U. S. Surgeon General
For juniors and seniors in health-related fields, and for students in programs of engineering and science. Funds in amounts to be determined by U. S. Surgeon General are available.

Write to
U. S. Surgeon General
U. S. Public Health Service
Washington, DC 20203
ATTN: Office of Personnel

Journalism, Communications and Drama

The Newspaper Fund
Any college junior interested in journalism in general and in newspaper work in particular is eligible. Recipient must work as reporter or copy editor on a U. S. newspaper. Internship is served between junior and senior years (summer), and scholarship is awarded in September following internship.

Write to
The Newspaper Fund
P. O. Box 300
Princeton, NJ 08540

William Randolph Hearst Foundation
Grants for study to undergraduate journalism students range from $75 to $100 per month.

Write to
William Randolph Hearst Foundation
3rd and Market Street
San Francisco, CA 94103

George Abbott Educational Foundation, Inc.
Established for students with talent in dramatic playwriting to attend the University of Rochester (N.Y.). Contact foundation for amounts.

Write to
George Abbott Educational Foundation, Inc.

234

630 Fifth Avenue
New York, NY 10020

American Newspaper Publishers Association Foundation
The foundation offers awards of varying amounts to black college students studying journalism.

Write to
American Newspaper Publishers Association Foundation
750 Third Avenue
New York, NY 10017

Harold E. Fellows Memorial Scholarship
$1,100 awarded to juniors in college.

Write to
National Association of Broadcasters
1771 N Street, N. W.
Washington, DC 20036

Law
Information Services

American Bar Association
1155 E. 60th Street
Chicago, IL 60637

NAACP Legal Defense and Educational Fund
10 Columbus Circle
New York, NY 10019

Scholarship Information Center
YMCA-YWCA, University of North Carolina
Chapel Hill, NC 27514

Executive Director
Council on Legal Educational Opportunity
Box 105, Morehouse College
Atlanta, GA 30314

Martin Luther King, Jr. Fellowship Program
Woodrow Wilson National Fellowship Foundation

Box 642
Princeton, NJ 08540

Medical and Allied Professions

American Fund for Dental Education
Pre-dental undergraduates in junior year are eligible for $2,500 for final year of undergraduate study and $2,500 for each year of regular dental school.

Write to
American Fund for Dental Education
211 E. Chicago Avenue
Chicago, IL 60611

National Institutes of Health
The NIH provides up to $1,500 renewable per academic year to nursing students.

Write to
U. S. Department of Health, Education & Welfare
National Institutes of Health
Student Loan and Scholarship Branch
9000 Raskille Parkway
Bethesda, MD 20014

American Medical Association
The AMA offers loans (of varying amounts) to students admitted to approved medical schools.

Write to
American Medical Association
Education and Research Foundation
535 No. Dearborn Street
Chicago, IL 60610

Beta Chi, Inc.
The group extends one scholarship of $500 for a girl to attend any accredited hospital school of nursing.

Write to
Beta Chi, Inc.
1211 Leeds Street
Utica, NY 13501

Bureau of State Services

Persons enrolled or accepted full-time in an accredited school of nursing having a loan fund under the Community Health Act may borrow up to $1,000 per academic year.

Write to
Bureau of State Services (Community Health)
U. S. Department of Health, Education & Welfare
Washington, DC 20201

The Community Health Act also establishes student loan funds for those pursuing degrees in medicine, dentistry, optometry or osteopathy. Students may obtain up to $2,000 per year.

Write to the addresses listed above.

Surgeon General

Funds in varying amounts are available for juniors and seniors in health-related fields and students in programs of engineering and science.

Write to
U. S. Surgeon General
U. S. Public Health Service
Washington, DC 20203
ATTN: Office of Personnel

National League for Nursing

The League offers funds in varying amounts for persons interested in nursing.

Write to
National League for Nursing
10 Columbus Circle
New York, NY 10019

Lever Brothers

The company provides fifty-one (one in each state and the District of Columbia) renewable $500 scholarships for pharmaceutical studies.

Write to
Public Relations Department
Lever Brothers
390 Park Avenue
New York, NY 10022

237

Additional Sources

Cooperative Admission and Aid Program
Awards are given to culturally disadvantaged youths upon recommendation of counselor.

Write to
Association of College Admissions Counselors
610 Church Street
Evanston, IL 60201

Eleanor Roosevelt Scholarship Program
Up to $1,500 per year is awarded to undergraduates actively involved in the civil rights movement.

Write to
Congress of Racial Equality
150 Nassau Street, Room 1312
New York, NY 10038

Elks of the World
The organization awards scholarships of varying amounts to black high school graduates.

Write to
Elks of the World
Imperial Lodge No. 127
160 W. 129th Street
New York, NY 10027

Herbert Lehman Fund
The fund offers aid in varying amounts to black undergraduate students.

Write to
Herbert Lehman Educational Fund
10 Columbus Circle, Suite 2030
New York, NY 10019

National Honor Society Scholarship Program
High school members of the National Honor Society should indicate desire for candidacy on the Preliminary Scholastic Aptitude Test (PSAT).

General Motors Scholarship Plan

The GM Corporation offers scholarships ranging from $200 to $2,000 per year for high school seniors.

Write to
General Motors Scholarship Plan
General Motors Building
Detroit, MI 48202

S & H Foundation, Inc. National Scholarship Program
Interested high school seniors should check item 10 on the Scholastic Aptitude Test (SAT), Code No. 0329. Award is $1,000 annually.

Westinghouse Science Talent Search
The fund is established for students interested in science careers. A high school science teacher should inquire.

Write to
Science Clubs of America
1719 N Street, N. W.
Washington, DC 20530

John McKee Scholarship Committee
Orphan boys in the Philadelphia area who are high school graduates not over eighteen years of age are eligible for these awards.

Write to
John McKee Scholarship Committee
643 Lawson Avenue
Havertown, PA 19183

National Association of Secondary School Principals
The association makes awards of $1,000 to senior members of the National Honor Society in respective high schools.

Write to
National Association of Secondary School Principals
1201 16th Street, N. W.
Washington, DC 20036

Pulitzer Scholarships
Seniors in public high schools in New York City must be nominated by their high school principals for these awards. Contact the principal

or

Write to
Pulitzer Scholarship, 202 Hamilton Hall

Columbia University
New York, NY 10027

General Mills, Inc.
The company offers awards in varying amounts to high school senior girls only.

Write to
General Mills, Inc.
9200 Wayzata Boulevard
Minneapolis, MN 55440

National 4-H Services Committee, Inc.
Currently enrolled and past members are eligible for grants up to $1,600. Not renewable.

Write to
National 4-H Services Committee, Inc.
59 E. Van Buren Street
Chicago, IL 60654

Armco Steel Corporation Community Scholarships
Students who rank in the top one-third of class and perform well on SAT are in line for renewable awards of $750. Student must live in a designated community in California, Kentucky, Maryland, Ohio, Missouri, Kansas, Oklahoma, Pennsylvania, Texas or West Virginia.

Write to
Armco Steel Corporation Community Scholarships
703 Curtis Street
Middleton, OH 45042

Ralph E. Smith Freedom Scholarships
Funds are valid for use at Macalester College. High school seniors may apply.

Write to
Macalester College
St. Paul, MN 55105

Sample Letter To Be Used in Applying for Financial Aid

```
                                  Street address
                                  City, state and zip code


                                  Date

Name and title (of Director of
   Financial Aid Program)
Name of Organization or Agency
City, state and zip code


Dear_____:
     (include Mr., Mrs. or Miss)

Please send me your application for financial assistance,
and any other information which you feel would be helpful
to me. I expect to graduate from _____
                                     (name of school)
in _____ in _____.
     (city and state)        (month and year)


Thank you for your attention to this request.

                                  Yours sincerely,



                                  _____
                                  (your signature)



                                  _____
                                  (name, printed or typed)
```

Note: Time is very important. Write for information at least a year ahead of the time you plan to enter school. Check the application deadlines carefully.

Medical and Health-Related Careers

Black Americans and other minorities have woefully inadequate health services available to them. One of the most severe problems in improving these services is inadequacy of medical manpower. So critical is the situation that the National Medical Association, an organization of black physicians, has established Project 75, a program to discover, develop and sustain interest in medicine and other health-related careers among black, Chicano, Indian and Puerto Rican students (the only ones under-represented in U. S. medical schools). Funded by the Office of Health Affairs, United States Office of Economic Opportunity, Project 75 offers a complete range of services— counseling, information about financial aid, tutoring, institutes, etc. A partial list of careers in the health-care field is listed below, but we recommend interested students to visit or write to Project 75 offices in their area. (Salaries mentioned may vary according to location.)

Write to
Project 75
National Office
1020 S. Wabash Avenue, Suite 700
Chicago, IL 60605

Project 75
Northeast Regional Office
2217 Fourth Street, NW
Washington, DC 20001

Project 75
Southeast Regional Office
985 Hunter Street, NW
Atlanta, GA 30314

Project 75
Rocky Mountain Regional Office
1899 Gaylord Street
Denver, CO 80206

Project 75
Pacific Coast Regional Office
1828 S. Western Avenue
Los Angeles, CA 90006

Training of One Year or Less after High School

Hospital Maintenance Engineer Assistant

Category includes carpenters, electricians, groundkeepers, painters, plumbers, masons, stationary engineers. Duties are repair, maintenance, upkeep of equipment, building and grounds, working under the supervision of hospital engineer. In-service training.

Inhalation Therapy Assistant

Administers oxygen to patients, checks on equipment and supplies of oxygen, keeps record of use of machines, etc. Three to nine months training in hospital. (See two-year courses in junior colleges, etc.) Salary is $85 weekly during training

Orthotist and Prosthetist

Works closely with physician, surgeon or therapist to provide rehabilitation for disabled. The *orthotist* makes and fits braces to correct physical defects. The *prosthetist* makes and fits artificial limbs. Both must have skill with hands and tools. High school sciences helpful. Hospital or shop apprenticeship for two years leads to apprenticeship. Four years on-the-job training plus examination leads to professional status. (See four-year special college training programs.) Salary is $5,000–$6,000 yearly as apprentice

Pediatric Aide

Assists nursing staff in care of children (feeding, bathing, supervising play). Six months in-service training is provided, with a salary of $65 weekly while training

Pharmacy Assistant

Under professional supervision, compounds routine pharmaceuticals, unpacks and sorts supplies, keeps stock, pre-packages weekly dosages. On-the-job training.

Physical Therapy Aide

Works under physical therapist. Usually enters as nurse's aide and then trains for a year under direction of physical therapist. Salary is $95 weekly while training

Training of Two Years after High School

Dental Assistant

Prepares for examination and treatment, sterilizes instruments, helps dentist, mixes fillings, helps in taking X-rays, answers phone, makes appointments, etc. Training involves one- or sometimes two-year courses, depending on training school. Some dentists train assistants on-the-job. (Two years training leads to certification.)

Histologic Technician

Cuts and stains body tissues for microscopic examination by pathologists. One-year supervised training in approved pathology laboratory, leading to certification exam. Salary is $110 weekly.

Junior Animal Lab Technician

Essentially an animal caretaker who works under professional direction, to understand basic characteristics and objectives of the research program. On-the-job training or one-year animal technician course plus one year's work experience leading to certification.

Licensed Practical Nurse

Care of the sick. Training takes 12 to 18 months—high school (some courses are part of high school curriculum) or 10th grade. Salary is $4,400 to $8,000.

Medical Assistant

Helps prepare patients for examinations, sterilizes instruments, takes temperatures, measures weight and heights, etc. May perform routine laboratory tests. Twelve months to two years special training at junior college or other school. Salary is $113 weekly.

Occupational Therapy Assistant

Works with occupational therapist, assisting in rehabilitating patients in hospitals or other health care facilities. Instructs patients in manual and creative arts, prepares materials and supplies, helps in maintaining tools and equipment. Usually one year training, conducted by hospitals or other health agencies leading to certification exam.

Training of Two to Three Years after High School

Accountant

Usually works under controller, prepares financial and statistical reports. Minimum training is two semesters of college level accounting or two years experience in hospital accounting. Salary is $125 weekly.

Cytotechnologist

Works under direction of a pathologist, screens slides of blood cells under microscope, tracing clues to diseases. Two years college training, including 12 semesters of biology, plus a minimum of one year of approved education and experience in cytotechnology, leading to a certification exam. (There is frequently no tuition charge in the last year, and there are some scholarships.) Salary is $5,500 annually.

Dental Hygienist

Cleans and polishes teeth, locates possible disease area for diagnosis by dentist, may take and develop x-rays, and generally assists dentist. (Primarily for women.) Usually two years training is required (there are some longer courses) plus state license. Salary is $6,000 annually.

Medical Laboratory Technician

Assists scientists by setting up equipment, performing routine chemical and physical tests, recording experimental results. Usually two years of junior college or other technical school is required with supervised clinical experience in approved laboratory. Salary is $6,000 annually.

Medical Illustrator

Uses drawings, painting, sculpture, photography for illustrating books, hospital charts, etc. At least two years training, including pre-medical studies as well as graphic technology, is necessary. Salary is $6,500 annually.

Mental Health Technician

Part of a treatment team in care, treatment and rehabilitation of mentally ill and mentally retarded patients. Works under direction of professional. Two years of training plus one summer of study, usually at junior college, are necessary. Salary is $6,500 annually.

Orthoptist

Helps overcome handicap of crossed eyes, using teaching techniques. Ususally assists opthalmologists in hospitals or clinics. Requires at least two years of college, plus two months practical work, before

245

enrolling in an approved training center for 10 to 12 months training. Leads to certification exam. (See also three- to four-year training description.)

Professional Nurse

Has overall responsibility for patient's nursing needs under direction of physician, with assistance of nurse's aides, practical nurses, etc. Usually begins as general duty nurse in hospital or clinic; can serve in doctor's office, private homes, as well as a public health nurse, etc (for men and women). An associate degree (two years training) in junior college leads to state examination for registered nurse. (See three- to four-year B.S. degree nursing program.) Salary is $6,000 annually.

Respiratory Therapist

Administers oxygen to patient, checks condition of equipment and supplies of oxygen. Keeps record of oxygen, etc.
Two years training at a junior college or other approved technical school is necessary. Salary is $6,000 annually.

Senior Animal Laboratory Technician

Helps in feeding, care, breeding of animals in research. Three years on the job or two years study at Animal Technology Laboratory School, plus one year's experience lead to certification.

X-Ray Technician

Helps physician by doing mechanical and routine work connected with X-ray use, taking pictures, keeping records, etc. Two years training in hospital or approved technical school leads to professional registration. Salary is $6,000 annually.

Training of Three to Four Years after High School

Medical Engineering Technician

Assembles, adapts, and maintains new devices and instruments. Four years training but new specialty courses may require less.

Medical Records Librarian

In charge of all classification material in hospital; indexes, catalogues of all information. Controls traffic of case records; prepares reports on request. Minimum of three years study (one year in hospital plus two years at college) or four-year program in an accredited college giving degrees in medical records administration. Salary is $6,500 annually.

Medical Technologist

Performs chemical, microscopic, bacteriological and other tests in laboratory under supervision of experienced physician or pathologist in hospital or clinical laboratory. Three years of college training, with emphasis on sciences, plus one year in hospital school of medical technology leading to certification. Salary is $7,000 annually.

Orthoptist

See two- to three-year section for description of duties. Some training schools require a college degree.

Orthotist and Prosthetist

See one year or less section for description of duties. There are some four-year B.S. degrees in these fields. Salary is $7,200 annually.

Professional Nurse

(See two- to three-year section for description of duties.) In addition to the two-year junior college programs, there are three-year nursing programs, usually in hospitals, as well as a four-year program with a B.S. degree, usually given at universities which have a medical school. All three lead to a registered nurse degree after passing the state examination. Those with higher education naturally are more likely to advance more quickly to become head nurses and supervisors. Salary ranges from $3,800 to $21,000 annually.

Programs for Veterans

Operation MEDIHC

MEDIHC stands for Military Experience Directed Into Health Careers. This is a cooperative effort by the Department of Health, Education, and Welfare and the Department of Defense, designed to assist the serviceman or woman trained in medical skills while in the service in finding a career in the health field upon return to civilian life. Persons who served in military fields unrelated to health, and who are interested in pursuing civilian health careers may also participate in Operation MEDIHC.

There is a growing shortage of qualified personnel in over 200 health fields in the United States. There are numerous job openings for health workers in hospitals, public health, research voluntary agencies, schools, and industry. MEDIHC can help qualified returning veterans to get started in health vocations that offer immediate income, or to get additional training if needed.

How MEDIHC Works
The MEDIHC program consists of three basic components: Identification, Counseling, and Placement.

Identification
Military installations obtain rosters of health-trained personnel from three to six months before separation. These individuals are contacted by their transition officer concerning participation in MEDIHC. Interested individuals fill out a Qualification/Referral Card outlining training, experience, job interest, and educational ambitions.

Counseling
The transition counselor appraises the individual's qualification, aptitudes, and interests and describes the opportunities available to him or her. The Qualification/Referral Cards are sent to U. S. Department of Health, Education and Welfare regional offices and from there directly to the MEDIHC Coordinator in the state designated by the ex-serviceman or woman.

Placement
The state coordinator assumes responsibility for placement. He makes sure that individuals hear from the institutions or facilities that have openings for which they qualify. At this point, each individual negotiates directly with an institution on specific terms of placement—salary, advancement opportunities, tuition, cost of training, or whatever other details are involved.

MEDEX

Medex is an innovative plan aimed at increasing the productivity of the medical practitioner. The project is aimed at strengthening that point in the system under the most strain: the primary care provider. Medex will develop an extension of the physician—in effect, another pair of hands available, under supervision, to help him 24 hours a day.
The first Medex program was developed in the state of Washington under the direction of Dr. Richard Smith, and has already graduated its first class. The program is continuing in Washington and is in the developmental stage in New Hampshire, North Dakota, Alabama and other states.

The Medex Training Program
The first urban Medex project has been awarded to the Department of

Community Medicine, Drew Postgraduate Medical School. For this purpose, the Drew School and the Los Angeles County—"Martin Luther King, Jr. General Hospital" are joined together to provide health manpower and services. The Medex demonstration program is divided into two phases: (1) a university training phase, and (2) a preceptorship phase.

Write to
Drew Postgraduate Medical School
Suite 204, 1635 East 103rd Street
Los Angeles, CA 90002

Colleges Offering Programs in Animal Technology

A number of colleges are now offering programs in animal technology. Some emphasize laboratory animal technology while others emphasize veterinary hospital technology. Included in the following list are a few schools that, while not currently offering programs, have these under consideration and may be made directly to the colleges of choice.

Two-year Programs
Write to
Animal Science Technology Department
Agricultural and Technical College
State University of New York
Delhi, NY 13753

Biological Technology Department
Laboratory Animal Technology Emphasis
Agricultural and Technical College
State University of New York
Farmingdale, NY 11735

Veterinary Medical Technology Department
Central Carolina Technical Institute
Sanford, NC 27330

Laboratory Animal Technology Program
College of Agriculture
Pennsylvania State University
University Park, PA 16802

Four-year Program
Write to
Veterinary Technology Program
Department of Animal Diseases

College of Agriculture
University of Connecticut
Storrs, CT 06268

Laboratory Animal Science Major
Department of Animal Science
Institute of Food and Agricultural Sciences
University of Florida
Gainesville, FL 32601

Laboratory Animal Science Program
College of Health Related Professions
State University of New York
Downstate Medical Center
450 Clarkson Avenue
Brooklyn, NY 11203

Biomedical Science Program
Department of Veterinary Public Health
College of Veterinary Medicine
Texas A & M University
College Station, TX 77843

Financial Aid Restricted to Health-Related Careers

American Association for
   Inhalation Therapy
3554 Ninth Street
Riverside, CA 92501
Inhalation therapy

American Association of Dental
Schools
211 E. Chicago Avenue
Chicago, IL 60611
Dentistry

American Association of
   H.P.E. & R.
1201 Sixteenth Street NW
Washington DC 20036
School nursing

American Association of Nurse
   Anesthetists
Suite 3010
Prudential Plaza
Chicago, IL 60601
Nurse anesthetics

American Chiropractic
   Association
Department of Information
   Services
2200 Grand Avenue
Des Moines, IA 50312
Chiropractics

250

The American Chiropractor
  Association
261 W. 71st Street
New York, NY 10023
Chiropractics

The American College of Hospital
  Administrators
850 North Lake Shore Drive
Chicago, IL 60610
Hospital administration

The American Dietetic Association
620 North Michigan Avenue
Chicago, IL 60611
Dietetics

American Fund for Dental
  Education
211 East Chicago Avenue
Chicago, IL 60611
**For predental undergraduates in
their junior year. $2,500 for
student's final year of
undergraduate predental study
and $2,500 for each year of the
four years of regular dental
school**

The American Medical
  Association
  Education and Research
  Foundation
535 N. Dearborn
Chicago, IL 60610
Medical educational training

American Occupational Therapy
  Association
251 Park Avenue South
New York, NY 10010
Occupational therapy

American Optometric Association
7000 Chippewa Street
St. Louis, MO 63119
Optometry

The American Orthoptic Council
3400 Massachusetts Avenue, N.W.
Washington, DC 20007
Orthoptic education

The American Osteopathic
  Association
Scholarship Committee, Chairman
212 East Ohio Street
Chicago, IL 60611
Osteopathy

American Pharmaceutical
  Association
2215 Constitution Avenue, N.W.
Washington, DC 20037
Pharmacy

The American Physical Therapy
  Association
1740 Broadway
New York, NY 10019
Physical therapy education

The American Physiological
  Society
9650 Rockville Pike
Bethesda, MD 20014
Physiology

American Podiatry Association
20 Chevy Chase Circle, NW
Washington, DC 20015
Podiatry

American Psychiatric Association
1700 - 18th Street, NW
Washington, DC 20009
Psychiatry

American Psychological
 Association
1200 - 17th Street, NW
Washington, DC 20036
Psychology

American Society for Microbiology
1913 I Street, NW
Washington, DC 20006
Bacteriology and microbiology

American Veterinary Medical
 Association
600 South Michigan Avenue
Chicago, IL 60605
Veterinary medicine

APA Committee on Scholarships
 and Fellowships
3301 16th Street, N.W.
Washington, DC 20010
**For college graduate to train a
minimum of two years in podiatry**

Army Careers
U. S. Army Recruiting Command
Hampton, VA 23369
**Walter Reed Army Institute
Nursing Programs for selected
high school graduates**

Atomic Energy Commission
c/o Fellowship Office
Oak Ridge Associated Universities
Oak Ridge, TN 37830
**For special fellowships in a nuclear
science and engineering, and health
physics**

Board of Laboratory Assistants
445 North Lake Shore Drive
Chicago, IL 60611
Laboratory assistants

Division of Training
Rehabilitation Service

Department of Health, Education,
and Welfare
Washington, DC 20201
**Medicine, dentistry, physical therapy,
speech pathology and audiology,
rehabilitation, nursing, prosthetics and
orthodontics, blind, deaf, and mentally
retarded and rehabilitation psychology**

Institute of Food Technologists
Scholarship Center
221 North LaSalle Street
Chicago, IL 60601
Food technology

The International Chiropractor
 Association
Columbia Institute of Chiropractics
New York, NY 10023
Chiropractics

Intersociety Committee on
Pathology Information
9650 Rockville Pike
Bethesda, MD 20014
Pathology

Kappa Kappa Gamma Fraternity
 Headquarters
530 East Town Street
Columbus, OH 43215
**Assists young women working
with mentally retarded, physically
handicapped, socially deprived,
emotionally disturbed or aged**

The Lockheed Leadership Fund
Emory University
Atlanta, GA 30322

Director of Admissions
Northwestern University
Evanston, IL 62201

Director of Admissions
Pomona College
Claremont, CA 91711

Director of Admissions
Harvard University
Cambridge, MA 02138

Director of Admissions
University of Southern California
Los Angeles, CA 90007
Five 4-year scholarships in aerospace medicine available.

Mead Johnson and Company
Evansville, IN 47721
Awards in pediatrics, general practice, administration, pharmacy and dietetics.

Medical Osteopathic Student
    Scholarships
The Surgeon-General
Department of the Navy
Washington DC 20390
(Attn: Code 3174)
The U.S. Navy offers scholarships for medical and osteopathic students classes of 1974, 1975, 1976). Full tuition, authorized fees, books ($200 per year), pay ($6,608, 16 to $10,821. 96 per annum), medical care (self and dependents). Four years of participation entails five years of active naval service after internship. Three years entails four years active service.

Medical Scholarships or Loan Funds
American Medical Association
535 North Dearborn Street
Chicago, IL 60610
Medical education loan program.

Medical Student and Resident
Assistance Foundation

Medical Student and Resident
Assistance Foundation
2000 Washington Street, Suite 323
Newton Lower Falls, MA 02162
ATTN: Dr. Jules Seletz
Available to juniors and seniors at Howard, Tufts and Boston Medical schools. May apply for loans up to approximately $2,500 per year.

Medical Technologists
P.O. Box 2544
Muncie, IN 47302
Medical technologists and cytotechnologists

National Association of Certified
    Dental Laboratories
3801 Mount Vernon Avenue
Alexandria, VA 22305
Dental laboratory technology

The National Easter Seal Society
for Crippled Children and Adults
2023 West Ogden Avenue
Chicago, IL 60612
Speech pathology and audiology (graduate level) physical and occupational therapy, special training in in minimal brain dysfunction (senior year in college)

The National Foundation March of
    Dimes
Suite 209
1028 Connecticut Avenue, N.W.
Washington, DC 20036
Health careers

National Medical Fellowships, Inc.
3935 Elm Street
Downers Grove, IL 65150
ATTN: Mrs. Hilde Reitz
Freshman and Sophomore Medical Students

253

New York Life Insurance Company
Career Information Service
Box 51, Madison Square Station
New York, NY 10017
Biologist education

New York Life Insurance Company
Medical Students Scholarship
    Program
Dean of Medicine
State University of New York
Albany, NY 12203
Medical scholarships

Division of Nursing
U. S. R. H. S.
Arlington, VA 22203
Nursing

National League for Nursing
10 Columbus Circle
New York, NY 10019
Nursing

Pennsylvania State University
Department of Biophysics
618 Life Sciences Building
University Park, PA 16802
Biophysicist

Registry of Medical Technologists
710 South Wolcott Avenue
Chicago, IL 60612
Cytotechnology

Alfred P. Sloan National
    Scholarships
Vanderbilt University
Wabash College
**Minimum of $200 to a normal maximum
of about $2,500. Medicine**

State Pharmacy Foundations
A number of state pharmacy
foundations have been organized
to provide financial assistance to
students entering a career in
pharmacy. For further information,
write to the college or pharmacy
of your choice.

Hattie M. Strong Foundation
Suite 407, Cafritz Building
1625 Eye Street, N.W.
Washington, DC 20006
Nursing

The Surgeon General, Department
    of the Army
ATTN-MEDPT-MP
Washington, DC 20315
**Dietetics, physical therapy and
occupational therapy**

The U. S. Public Health Service,
    Career Development Review
    Branch
Division of Research Grants,
    National Institute of Health
Bethesda, MD 20014
**Public health traineeships, psychiatric–
mental health, professional nurse, nurse
scientist graduate, nursing research,
health, medical and related biological
sciences, and U. S. Army and Navy**

U. S. Public Health Service
    Traineeships
Office of the Chairman,
    Department of Health Care
    Administration
George Washington University
Washington, DC 20006

Tips on Applying for Financial Aid

1. If you are applying to a college and will need financial assistance, mention your need at the time of application.

2. When writing for information about financial assistance, regardless of source, be clear and include information on the timing involved.

3. If you call for information, or in case of any telephone contact with a financial assistance source, make a note of the name of the person spoken with, the department in which he or she is located, telephone extension number and the date of the conversation.

4. Comply with deadlines when making application for financial assistance.

5. Examine your application carefully to be sure that all questions have been correctly answered, or that you have entered "N.A." (not applicable) in the proper spaces.

6. If it is impossible to contact a person before using his name as a reference, be sure to inform him as soon as possible afterward.

7. Check that your application is properly signed, and that the supporting documents requested are enclosed.

8. If you cannot obtain all of the documents requested prior to the deadline for submitting your application, submit the application and notify the funding source of your problem. It is helpful to list the documents you are unable to obtain; the approximate date documents will be available; the earliest date documents can be expected to reach funding source.

9. After you have submitted your application, allow a reasonable amount of time for processing before you make inquiry. Frequent inquiries often hinder processing, especially in large offices.

10. Promptly acknowledge and answer follow-up inquiries made to you about your application.

11. Notify source immediately if your address changes.

12. Check to see if the school or other source to which you are applying requiries a Parents' Confidential Statement. If so, P.C.S. forms may be obtained from high school or college counselors, the College Examination Board, or the Health Careers Program office.

Financial Aid
Restricted to Minorities

Catholic Scholarship for Negroes, Inc.
For high school seniors (not limited to Catholics). Applications must be made in the fall for consideration for the following school year.

Write to
Mrs. Roger L. Putnam, President
Catholic Scholarships for Negroes, Inc.
254 Union Street
Springfield, MA 01105

Cooperative Program, Educational Opportunity
For high school seniors. Major part of the program focuses on blacks. Students admitted to program receive necessary amount of financial aid

Write to
Director of Indian Education
Write to
Cooperative Program, Education Opportunity
17 Hill House Avenue
New Haven, CT 06520

Director of Indian Education
Minnesota students of at least one-fourth Indian ancestry attending advanced or specialized education in accredited or approved college, business, technical or vocational schools are eligible for tuition, incidental fees, and room and board not to exceed $800 per academic year for four years.
Centennial Building
St. Paul, MN 55101

Ford Foundation
Doctoral fellowships for black students.

Write to
Ford Foundation
Doctoral Fellowships for Black Students
320 East 43rd Street
New York, NY 10017

Manhattan College Scholarship
For black students at Manhattan College. Amounts up to tuition costs each year.

Write to
Manhattan College Scholarship
Financial Aid Office
Manhattan College
Bronx, NY 10471

Martin Luther King Memorial Scholarship

For black students. Tuition, plus several hundred dollars for miscellaneous expenses.

Write to
Martin Luther King Memorial Scholarship
Financial Aid Department
University of Southern California
Los Angeles, CA 90024

Martin Luther King Jr. Scholarship Fund

For minority students, both graduates and undergraduates—awarded according to financial need.

Write to
Martin Luther King Jr. Scholarship Fund
Office of Admissions and Financial Aid
New York University
13 University Place
New York, NY 10003

Minority Groups Scholarship Program

For high school seniors attending the following colleges: Antioch, Carleton, Grinnell, Oberlin, Occidental, Reed, Swarthmore. Amounts awarded vary.

Write to
Admission Officer of the particular member college

National Achievement and Scholarship Program for Outstanding Negro Students

High school seniors, apply through your high school principal or guidance counselor. ($1,000-$6,000 scholarships for four years.)

Write to
National Achievement and Scholarship Program for Outstanding Negro Students
900 Grove Street
Evanston, IL 60201

National Scholarship Service and Fund for Negro Students

Applicant must receive some counseling from NSSFNS.

Write to
National Scholarship Service and Fund for Negro Students
1776 Broadway
New York, NY 10019

257

Rockefeller Foundation

Scholarship aid for disadvantaged students, (graduates of Southern high schools), not exclusively a program for black students.

Write to

Duke University, Durham, North Carolina; Emory University, Atlanta, Georgia; Tulane University, New Orleans, Louisiana; Vanderbilt University, Nashville, TN.

State Board for Indian Scholarships

Ten scholarships of $1,500 per year are awarded each year for resident persons of at least one-fourth Indian ancestry to attend any institution of higher learning in North Dakota. Students must demonstrate financial need.

Write to

State Board for Indian Scholarships
Director of Indian Education
Department of Public Instruction
State of North Dakota
Bismarck, ND 58501

United Negro College Fund

Grants are available for the first year of graduate study

Write to

United Negro College Fund
22 East 54th Street
New York, NY 10022

John Hay Whitney Foundation

Primarily for racially or culturally deprived students. Must be a college senior about to begin graduate work. $3,000 yearly maximum.

Write to

John Hay Whitney Foundation
111 West 50th Street
New York, NY 10020

Financial Aid Restricted to Regions

The Hartford Foundation

Interracial Scholarships Committee of Greater Hartford. Restricted to residents of Hartford, Connecticut.

Write to

The Hartford Foundation

258

Station for Public Giving
621 Farmington Avenue
Hartford, CT 06105

The Public Schools of the District of Kansas City, Missouri
Special scholarship program restricted to residents of Kansas City, Mo.

Mabel Wilson Richards Scholarship Fund
For needy and worthy girls living in the Los Angeles area. Apply
through scholarship office of specified medical schools in California, or

Write to
Mabel Wilson Richards Scholarship Fund
1977 DeMille Drive
Los Angeles, CA 90027

Model Cities Scholarships
Model Cities Scholarships are restricted to residents of the Model Cities
area in each particular city. However, students may attend any
accredited post-secondary school anywhere in the United States.
For D.C. residents, $200,000 has been made available for students in
Model City area no. 6, south of Howard University. The top scholarship
will be $1,000. Top priority will be given to Washington Technical
Institute, Federal City College, Howard University and D.C. Teachers'
College applicants.

Write to
Mr. Robert McCormack
D.C. Department of Human Resources
1329 E Street NW
Washington DC 20004
or
The National Medical Association Foundation Health Careers Program
Washington, DC 20005

National Medical Association Foundation
Restricted to applicants from the Los Angeles area. Both scholarship
and loan program for students in health or health-related careers.

Write to
National Medical Association Foundation
Health Careers Program
1635 East 103rd Street
Los Angeles, CA 90002

Grand Street Boys' Foundation

Grants for residents of New York City who need further financial assistance after receiving maximum loans from New York State Higher Education Assistance Corporation and Federal loans.

Write to
Grand Street Boys Foundation
131 West 56th Street
New York, NY 10019

Ohio State Medical Association

Ohio residency and admission to an approved medical school are required. Two $500 four-year scholarships are awarded annually.

Write to
Ohio State Medical Association
Committee on Rural Health
17 South High Street
Columbus, OH 43215

Educational and Scientific Trust of the Pennsylvania Medical School

One-year tuition scholarships are awarded to ten first-year students who are residents of Pennsylvania entering Pennsylvania medical schools. Half-tuition scholarships are awarded to upperclassmen.

Write to
Educational and Scientific Trust of the Pennsylvania Medical Society
Taylor Bypass and Erford Road
Lemoyne, PA 17043

National Medical Association Foundation

Scholarship and loan programs for students in health or health-related careers. Financial assistance is restricted primarily to applicants in the Washington, D.C., area. Special funding in limited amounts is available for students on a national basis. All participants may attend any accredited post-secondary school or training program.

Write to
National Medical Association Foundation
Health Careers Program
1013 12th Street, N.W.
Washington, DC 20005

Financial Aid: Loans

American Medical Association Education and Research Foundation

Applicant must have completed first term of medical school. Apply through medical school financial aid officer. Up to $1500 per year.

Write to
American Medical Association Education
535 North Dearborn Street
Chicago, IL 60610

State of Alabama Board of Medical Scholarship Awards

Maximum $2,000 per year, or $8,000 over a four-year period. Restricted to residents of Alabama who have been accepted for matriculation by the Medical College of Alabama, or a comparable institution.

Write to
State of Alabama Board of Medical Scholarship Awards
Scholarship Awards
1919 Seventh Avenue, South
Brimingham, Alabama 35233

American Medical Women's Association, Inc.

Maximum $1,000 per year. Available to women who are U.S. citizens enrolled in a U.S. medical school.

Write to
American Medical Women's Association, Inc.
1750 Broadway
New York, NY 10019

Bergen Foundation

Nursing loans. Usually covers tuition costs for high school graduates or girls who are in nursing school.

Write to
Bergen Foundation
6536 Sunset Boulevard
Hollywood, CA 90028

Eddy Student Loan Fund

Up to $1,500 a year for college juniors and seniors, or a student who just completed two years of work at an accredited college.

Write to
Eddy Student Loan Fund
c/o Thomas and Thomas
504 Broadway
Suite 1016
Gary, IN 64602

Educational and Scientific Trust of the Pennsylvania Medical Society

Available to Pennsylvania residents attending medical schools in the United States.

Write to
Educational and Scientific Trust of the Pennsylvania Medical Society
Taylor Bypass and Erford Road
Lemoyne, PA 17043

Educational Fund, Inc.

From $700 to $14,000 over a four-year period. High School students and college students.

Write to
Educational Fund, Inc.
10 Dorance Street
Providence, RI 02901

Entrenous Club of Detroit

Maximum $200 per quarter. Student must be matriculated at Wayne State U. Preference is given to black students.

Write to
Entrenous Club of Detroit
Student Loan Fund
Office of Scholarship and Financial Aid
Wayne State University
Detroit, MI 48202

Fellows Memorial Fund

Generous loans provided for medical, nursing, or theological students who are bona fide residents of one of the four counties of northwestern Florida and who intend to practice in that region.

Write to
Fellows Memorial Fund
c/o President, Pensacola Junior College
1000 College Boulevard
Pensacola, FL 32504

Friends Education Fund

For black students. Must be used at Indiana colleges and universities.

Write to
Friends Education Fund

262

F.E.F.F.N.
1004 State Office Building
Indianapolis, IN 46204

Funds for Education, Inc.
Loans from $350 to $2,500 for use at any school, college or university.

Write to
Funds for Education, Inc.
319 Lincoln Street
Manchester, NH 01201

The Health Professions Loan Program
Careers in medicine, dentistry, osteopathy, optometry, pharmacy and podiatry.

Write to
The Health Professions Loan Program
Bureau of Health Manpower
U.S. Public Health Service
National Institutes of Health - Bldg. 31
9000 Rockville Pike
Bethesda, MD 20014

W. K. Kellogg Foundation
Available for full-time graduate students in hospital administration at George Washington University.

Write to
W. K. Kellogg Foundation
Hospital Administration Loan Fund
Office of Student Financial Aid
George Washington University
Washington, DC 20006

National Association of Colored Women
Amounts vary.

Write to
National Association of Colored Women
1601 R Street, N.W.
Washington, DC 20009

New York Higher Education
Full-time students may borrow up to $1,000 for the freshman year, $1,000 for the sophomore year, $1,250 the third year, and $1,500 the

263

fourth and subsequent years of school. Maximum amount for any one student is $7,500. Students may borrow from any lending institution in the State of New York which participates in the Student Loan Program.

Write to
New York Higher Education
Assistance Corporation
159 Delaware Avenue
Delmar, NY 12054

Henry Warren Roth Education Fund
May be applied for by all undergraduate students.

Write to
Henry Warren Roth Education Fund
Financial Aid Office
Theil College
Greenville, PA 16125

Hattie M. Strong Loan Foundation
From $800 to $1,500 available for graduating high school seniors.

Write to
Hattie M. Strong Loan Foundation
409 Cafritz Building
1625 I Street, N.W.
Washington, DC 20006

The Tuition Plan
Loans regardless of location of school.

Write to
The Tuition Plan
410 North Michigan Avenue
Chicago, IL 60611

United Student Aid Fund
Loans up to $1,000 for graduates and undergraduates of any of the 700 participating schools.

Write to
United Student Aid Fund
845 3rd Avenue
New York, NY 10022

Career Opportunities in the Military Services

An extraordinarily wide variety of career opportunities is available for those persons who wish to join one of the United States military services, the ROTC or the reserves. The U. S. Air Force, for example, offers 6,500 college scholarships that cover tuition, laboratory and incidental fees, and a textbook allowance. In addition, each air force cadet gets $100 a month tax free as a personal allowance. Air Force ROTC offers free flying lessons as a separate incentive. In the U.S. Army, there are some 200 courses available, ranging from those for training of radio operators to those for motor transport specialists, medical personnel and law enforcement. The army offers $307.20 a month to start, plus regular raises and promotions and other incentives. In the U.S. Navy, one can take advantage of training in medicine, dentistry, electronics, communications and numerous other fields, and there are two Navy Scholarship Programs and an Enlisted Program for men and women interested in one of more than 50 skills. In the Army Reserve there are some 300 career training opportunities, depending on the specific skill requirements of a local unit, and these may range from electronics to finance to communications. After four or more months of basic and advanced training, the individual enrolls in the school that fits his plans and ambitions. A 63-page booklet which fully explains military career opportunities and lists numerous advanced educational programs is available free from: Director, Department of Defense High School News Service (Basic Facts Edition), Building 1-B, Great Lakes, IL 60088. For additional information

Write to
Army Opportunities
P.O. Box 5510
Philadelphia, PA 19143
Information also available for Army Reserve and ROTC

Air Force Academy
Box A
Randolph Air Force Base, TX 78148
Information also available for Air Force ROTC

The New Navy
Navy Yard, Building 157–4
Washington, DC 20390
Information also available for Naval ROTC

Careers Without College

In spite of the fact that many more occupations than before now stress college degees, there are some employment areas that do not require a four-year liberal arts background. Some special training is usually required, but the educational foundation for many excellent jobs can be obtained from technical-vocational programs in high schools, post-high school technical-vocational schools and technical departments in junior, community and four-year institutions. Be sure to contact the high school guidance counselor and the state director of vocational education; they have the most comprehensive information on careers without college. Also be sure to check the scholarships and financial aid section in this book, for many states have grant programs for use at technical-vocational schools.

The occupations listed below reflect two very important trends: first, they do not require a college degree, and second, they are listed in the *Occupational Outlook Handbook* 1972–73 edition, published by the U.S. Department of Labor, Bureau of Labor Statistics, Bulletin 1700, U.S. Government Printing Office, Washington, D.C. 20402, price $6.25 (an excellent resource found in the public library) as needing many new employees in the coming years. We have listed these fields and where to write for more information.

Air-conditioning, Refrigeration and Heating Mechanics
Write to

Refrigeration Service Engineers Society
433 North Waller Avenue
Chicago, IL 60644

Education Department
National Oil Fuel Institute
60 E. 42nd Street
New York, NY 10017

Appliance Servicemen
Write to

Association of Home Appliance Manufacturers
20 N. Wacker Drive
Chicago, IL 60606

Gas Appliance Manufacturers Association
1901 N. Fort Myer Drive
Arlington, VA 22209

National Appliance and Radio-Television Dealers Association
318 W. Randolph Street
Chicago, IL 60601

Building Trades
Asbestos workers, bricklayers, carpenters, cement masons,

266

electricians, elevator constructors, glaziers, lathers, marble setters, terrazzo setters, tile setters, painters, paper hangers, pipefitters, plasterers, plumbers, roofers, sheet-metal workers, stonemasons, structural iron workers, rodmen.

Write to
AFL-CIO
Building and Construction Trades
Department
815 16th Street, NW
Washington, DC 20006

Business Machine Servicemen
Contact local business machine dealers, or the state employment service for programs under the Manpower Development and Training Act.

Commercial Artists
Write to
National Art Education
Association
1201 16th Street, NW
Washington, DC 20036

Computer Operating Personnel
Write to
Data Processing Management
Association
505 Busse Highway
Park Ridge, IL 60068

Computer Programmers
Write to
Data Processing Management
Association
505 Busse Highway
Park Ridge, IL 60068

American Federation of
Information Processing Societies
210 Summit Avenue
Montvale, NJ 07645

Cosmetologists
Write to
National Beauty Career Center
3839 White Plains Road
Bronx, NY 10467

National Hairdressers and
Cosmetologists Association
3510 Olive Street
St. Louis, Missouri 63103

Dental Assistants
Write to
American Dental Assistants
Association
211 E. Chicago Avenue
Chicago, IL 60611

Division of Dental Health
Public Health Service
Department of Health, Education &
Welfare
Washington, DC 20201

Dental Laboratory Technicians
Write to
American Dental Association
Council on Dental Education
211 E. Chicago Avenue
Chicago, IL 60611

National Association of Certified
Dental Laboratories, Inc.
3801 Mt. Vernon Avenue
Alexandria, VA 22305

Diesel Mechanics
Write to
International Association of
Machinists & Aerospace Workers
1300 Connecticut Avenue, N. W.
Washington, DC 20036

Sheet Metal Workers' International
Association
1000 Connecticut Avenue, NW
Washington, DC 20036

Draftsmen
Write to
American Institute for Design and
Drafting
P. O. Box 2955
Tulsa, OK 74101

American Federation of Technical
Engineers
1126 16th Street, NW
Washington, DC 20036

Engineering and Science
Technicians
Write to
American Society for Engineering
Education
Suite 400
1 Dupont Circle
Washington, DC 20036

National Council of Technical
Schools
1835 K Street, NW
Room 907
Washington, DC 20006

Engineers' Council for
Professional Development
345 E. 47th Street
New York, NY 10017

Food Processing Technicians
Write to
National Council of Technical
Schools
1835 K Street, NW
Room 907
Washington, DC 20006

Forestry Aids
Write to
U. S. Department of Agriculture
Forest Service
Washington, DC 20250

Hospital Attendants
Write to
Division of Careers and
Recruitment
American Hospital Association
840 N. Lake Shore Drive
Chicago, IL 60611

Industrial Machinery Repairmen
Write to
International Association of
Machinists & Aerospace Workers
1300 Connecticut Avenue, NW
Washington, DC 20036

Instrument Makers
Write to
International Association of
Machinists & Aerospace Workers
1300 Connecticut Avenue, NW
Washington, DC 20036

National Machine Tool Builders
Association
2139 Wisconsin Avenue, NW
Washington, DC 20007

Instrument Repairmen
Write to

National Tool, Die & Precision
Machining Association
1411 K Street, NW
Washington, DC 20005

269

Instrument Society of America
530 William Penn Pl.
Pittsburgh, PA 15200

Scientific Apparatus Makers
Association
Process Measurement & Control
Section
370 Lexington, Avenue
New York, NY 10017

**Interior Designers and
Decorators**
Write to
National Society of Interior
Designers, Inc.
315 E. 62nd Street
New York, NY 10021

Library Technicians
Write to
American Library Association
50 E. Huron Street
Chicago, IL 60611

Licensed Practical Nurses
Write to
ANA-NLN Committee on Nursing
Careers
American Nurses' Association
10 Columbus Circle
New York, NY 10019

National Federation of Licensed
Practical Nurses, Inc.
250 W. 57th Street
New York, NY 10019

Lithography Occupations
Write to
Lithographers & Photoengravers
International Union
233 W. 49th Street
New York, NY 10019

Graphic Arts Technical
Foundation
4615 Forbes Avenue
Pittsburgh, PA 15213

Medical Assistants
Write to
American Association of Medical
Assistants
200 E. Ohio Street
Chicago, IL 60611

American Medical Association
Council on Medical Education
535 N. Dearborn Street
Chicago, IL 60610

**Occupational Therapy
Assistants**
Write to
The American Occupational
Therapy Association
251 Park Avenue
New York, NY 10010

Optometric Assistants
Write to
American Optometric Association
7000 Chippewa Street
St. Louis, MO 63119

**Photographic Laboratory
Occupations**
Write to
Master Photo Dealers' and
Finishers' Association
603 Lansing Avenue
Jackson, MI 49202

Professional Photographers of
America, Inc.
1090 Executive Way
Des Plaines, Illinois 60018

Physical Therapy Assistants
Write to
The American Physical Therapy
Association
1156 15th Street, N. W.
Washington, DC 20005

Technologists
Write to
The American Society of
Radiologic Technologists
645 N. Michigan Avenue
Chicago, IL 60611

The American Registry of
Radiologic Technologists
2600 Wayzata Boulevard
Minneapolis, MN 55405

Surgical Technicians
Write to
Association of Operating Room
Technicians, Inc.
8085 E. Prentice
The Denver Technological Center
Englewood, CO 80110

271

Surveyors
Write to
American Congress on Surveying
and Mapping
Woodward Building
733 15th Street, N. W.
Washington, DC 20005

Television & Radio
Service Technicians
Write to
National Alliance of Television
Associations
5908 S. Troy Street
Chicago, IL 60629

Also contact the state employment office for training under the
Manpower Development and Training Act.

Welders, Oxygen & Arc
Cutters
Write to

The American Welding Society
345 E. 47th Street
New York, NY 10017

International Brotherhood of
Boilermakers, Iron Shipbuilders,
Blacksmiths, Forgers and Helpers
8th at State Avenue
Kansas City, KS 66101

Index
Volume I

Volume III

277